W9-BLN-480

The music of **Stockhausen**

MD
MD
KD
M(d)
Momente

The music of Stockhausen

an introduction by **Jonathan Harvey**

University of California Press
Berkeley and Los Angeles 1975

University of California Press
Berkeley and Los Angeles, California

ISBN: 0-520-02311-0
Library of Congress Catalog Card Number: 72-85531

Printed in Great Britain

Contents

Acknowledgements

I would like to acknowledge the kind help and unstinting generosity of Universal Edition, who lent me scores and supplied information, of Hugh Davies and Richard Toop who gave me many insights into Stockhausen's mind in the course of two short afternoons in addition to which Richard Toop subsequently supplied much helpful material, of Alexander Goehr and our composer-students at Southampton in 1970–71 with whom there were discussions too numerous to mention, of William Kimber who asked me to write the book, of Judith Osborne who made many editorial suggestions, of Stockhausen who read it and made several corrections, and above all of Rosaleen, my wife, who copied out vast tracts of my scribble (amongst other things), and without whom nothing . . .

The publishers gratefully acknowledge the following for permission to quote music examples: Universal Edition (London) Ltd., for works by Stockhausen and Messiaen; Universal Edition (A. A. Kalmus Ltd.) for the piece by Webern.

1
Background

Karlheinz Stockhausen was born in an extreme era of human history. His first years were influenced by economic depression and the nadir of the German morale, and at the age of four, in January 1933, perhaps at the time of his first dawning impressions of the outside world, he saw the birth of the Third Reich, the swing of the sick German spirit from depressive to manic. The background is worth sketching, not because I pretend to draw any conclusions about Stockhausen's strange personality from it – such conclusions would almost certainly have to be depth-psychological to have any validity beyond the superficial – but because many of his statements, personal philosophies, and even the music, become more intelligible to us who have not gone through such extreme climates when they are placed in this perspective. For instance, he said recently: 'I had no reason to trust any adult, because they would change with the change of the system and compromise with any new situation. I found that ideology was something I couldn't rely on, and that I should attach myself to the divine. Of my own choice I first became a *practising* Catholic ... I was 17 or 18.'* Or, on the musical side, his dislike of regular rhythm, which reminds him of Nazi radio,† and consequent preference for rhythms in which the 'players are floating freely'.

The extreme nature of the political climate of Germany dates back to the First World War, perhaps beyond. The democratic, moderate centre of the Weimar Republic was only occasionally able to form an adequate parliamentary majority out of its own strength without the help of the extremists. The Socialist-Communist Left on the one hand and the Nazi Right on the other were openly hostile to this weak-kneed fruit of defeat with its reparations and its glaring social inequalities, and dreamed either of the militaristic splendour of the Hohenzollern Monarchy – the 'new dictator' Richard Strauss was always talking about – or something more on the lines of revolutionary Russia. (Stockhausen's geographical area, incidentally, was, half a year before the collapse of the Weimar Republic and of all factions other than the Nazis, notably anti-Nazi; the polls of July 1932 show that Cologne-Aachen was stubbornest of all in its resistance to the Nazi advance.)

* Interview with Stockhausen: 'Spiritual Dimensions', *Music and Musicians*, May 1971, p. 38.

† *Ibid.*, p. 39.

The Republic tottered through the miseries of inflation in 1923, a subsequent unreal five years of prosperity and savage profiteering based on some seven hundred and fifty million of foreign, largely American, loans, and finally the collapse of Wall Street in October 1929, which has been described as the most serious world economic crisis since the dawn of the industrial era. Millions were thrown out of a job and on the same impulse Hitler was thrown into business. He promised jobs and bread, the controlling of the tycoons (especially the Jewish ones), the end of corruption, the Versailles Treaty and reparations, the restoration of a national pride – as extreme as had been the preceding national humiliation – and a sense of purpose.

The general exhilaration and sense of enthusiasm was very striking in the years after the Nazis' ascendancy to power in 1933. Observers were astonished to see that, despite the sinister Gestapo, the concentration camps, the ruthless Blood Purge of 1934, the censorship and regimentation, the man in the street was happy with the new regime.* The Jews, the communists, the pacifists and individualists, like 'the past', were reduced to inconspicuousness or eliminated. The university professors, amongst whom one might have expected considerable opposition to Nazism, were in Weimar days 'anti-liberal, anti-democratic and anti-Semitic' and, though before '33 suspicious of the rowdy nature of the Nazis, were largely quite happy with the new dictatorship when it settled in. There were, of course, honourable exceptions who fled or suffered, as well as all the ordinary decent men and women who were understandably terrified to step publicly an inch out of line, and, of course, the Jews who had no choice, who just *were* out of line whatever their political views.

The exhilarating togetherness of the new Germans seemed much more important than old notions of individualistic thought; the new issues seemed too urgent. The universities began to teach *German* physics, *German* chemistry, and a journal started in 1937 called *Deutsche Mathematik* spoke about the dangers of not bringing racialism into mathematics – this carried 'within itself the germs of the destruction of German science'. The highly respected Professor Philipp Lenard of Heidelberg University wrote: 'German Physics? "But," it will be replied, "science is and remains international." It is false. In reality, science like every other human product, is racial and conditioned by blood.' The arts faculties seemed to be dominated by courses on *Rassenkunde* – racial science – history was rewritten and books were burnt.

The students too were aglow with the new ideals. And even more was the Hitler Youth, with its ordered stages like a nightmarish Boy Scout movement – looking after children from six to eighteen, at which age they had to serve in the Labour Service and the Army. By the end of 1938 the movement numbered nearly eight million. The four million who had evaded it, despite prison sentences for recalcitrant parents, were compulsorily conscripted in March 1939, though the new law did not manage to operate fully. These youths, whose

* William L. Shirer, *The Rise and Fall of the Third Reich*, Secker and Warburg, London, 1960, p. 231.

ideological growth was carefully noted in their performance book, passed tests at the age of ten in athletics, camping and Nazified history, and took the following graduation oath: 'In the presence of this blood banner, which represents our Fuehrer, I swear to devote all my energies and my strength to the saviour of our country, Adolf Hitler. I am willing and ready to give up my life for him, so help me God.'

With their poisoned minds and beautiful healthy bodies, these boys and girls radiated a joy that impressed and thrilled the world. As Count Harry Kessler wrote, 'we (especially in Germany) have turned towards the Greeks in many ways but nowadays, in contrast to the classicists, quite unconsciously and naturally as part of real life. Nudity, light, sunshine, the adoration of living, bodily completeness and sensuousness without false shame or prudery. It is really astounding how the bodies, the physical vitality of young people have obeyed this drive, and how much more beautiful they are now [1930] than they were before the War. It is a blossoming of the whole body of the people since human beings lost their shame of being naked. Maillol [the Parisian artist] asked me to photograph two young people who were, as he said, "beaux comme les dieux antiques".'*

As is well known, those who had ideas of their own, faiths of their own or who simply didn't like crowds were not so happy. They were the outsiders who ceased to impinge on the consciousness of the average man: almost irrelevant to a true picture of German consciousness at that time, with its daily censorship of papers, radio, books, films and plays. In the case of religion, there was little overt protest over the arresting of several thousand pastors and priests. Rosenberg's, Bormann's and Himmler's aim was to eradicate Christianity and resuscitate old Wotan and his fellows in Nordic deity. They had Hitler's full backing. Rosenberg's new thirty articles stipulated that the new National Church would have no priests, only National Reich orators; no Bibles, crucifixes or pictures of saints to be left in place; instead *Mein Kampf* ('the greatest of all documents', 'to the German nation and therefore to God the most sacred book'), a sword, and in the crucifix's place the swastika. Thus the buildings which had housed 'the strange and foreign Christian faiths imported into Germany in the ill-omened year 800' were to be converted. The extremism of a regime with these feelings in its blood is hard to exaggerate.

In the case of the arts, the suppression of modernism, foreign influence, the Jews and everything else inimical to what was essentially a popular anti-intellectual movement had its usual by now drearily familiar results. The speeches of Dr. Goebbels, the propaganda minister, were full of 'inspired' nationalism, of gathering together 'the creative artists in all spheres into a unified organisation under the leadership of the Reich', as his Reich Chamber of Culture articles put it. As in Maoist China and the Soviet Union, the results were dismal. Hitler took a personal interest in the purification of the visual arts and removed some 6,500 'modern' paintings by Kokoschka, Grosz,

* As recounted in his diary 'In the Twenties' reprinted in translation in *Encounter*, September 1967, p. 23.

Cézanne, Van Gogh, Gauguin, Matisse and Picasso from the art galleries; he selected personally nine hundred paintings for an exhibition of Nazi art, put his jack boot through others and delivered a lengthy speech of which the following is an excerpt: 'Works of art that cannot be understood but need a swollen set of instructions to prove their right to exist and find their way to neurotics who are receptive to such stupid or insolent nonsense will no longer openly reach the German nation.' Schirer reports that in Munich at least, where Goebbels organised an exhibition of 'degenerate art' (impressionist and expressionist works mainly) to show the people from what they were being saved, the people were not so overjoyed with the new way, and much to Goebbels' fury and embarrassment flocked to the exhibition in such numbers that he hastily closed it.

Third Reich theatre was a complete write-off, overtly Nazi with its 'blood and soil' dramas of the good earth and peasant life, and its historical dramas extolling German heroes of one sort or another. This is not to say that masterpieces of the past were not performed, they were, as they were in music.

The opulence of music in the era was as striking as was the stifling of the new. Schoenberg left, Hindemith's works were forbidden, Berg and Webern were for the most part ignored (Berg only lived to see two years of the Third Reich; his international reputation was achieved before it became a relevant factor). But Strauss became president of Goebbels's Reich Music Chamber, and together with Wagner and the great German tradition received excellent and abundant performances from the many gifted musicians who flourished under the regime.

Joel Sachs has shown* that aggressive nationalism and conservatism as a major force in German music dates from well before 1933, if not from Wagner's notorious explosion 'Judaism in Music' of 1850. Music such as Schoenberg's Five Orchestral Pieces Op. 16 (1909) was just the last straw in the load of 'International Jewry, Bolshevism, "Niggerising" (*Verniggerung*) Anglo-French conspiracies to destroy German culture' which broke the back of the paranoiac bourgeois musician. Vitriolic articles proliferated, and in 1933 all those years of campaigning and denigration paid off, and the heads rolled.

What effect the war itself might have had on a youth aged eleven to seventeen, the shock in Cologne of experiencing the first British one-thousand-plane bombing in 1942, the trauma of defeat, guilt and confusion which the German spirit must have felt at the end of the war, the rumours of what Hitler's New Order had been doing to the conquered Slavs and Jews, is beyond imagination. We who were not a part of it find it beyond the powers of human imagination and comprehension, so how much deeper below the powers of conscious comprehension must it have struck in those who lived through it. No wonder the German youth of today is often cut off from the past and buried in 'the relevant' in a way others can hardly credit. They too reach for their revolver when they hear the word *Kultur*.

---

* 'Some aspects of musical politics in Pre-Nazi Germany' in *Perspectives of New Music*, vol. 9, no. 1, pp. 74–95.

Background

For a barometer as sensitive as Stockhausen, these years of historic extremism cannot have been without fundamental impact, though his creative life, as opposed to his formative life, has been lived in a time of reconstruction, a time of starting anew with a clean slate.

For those who like history in neat packages, 1950 is a fairly accurate landmark. The dust of the war had settled, the first fruits of Messiaen's post-war teaching were beginning to ripen in Europe, and modern music festivals or courses such as the Donaueschinger Musiktage and the Darmstadt Internationale Ferienkurse für Neue Musik were starting or resuming operations. A whole new surface was applied to music. It was described and analysed in terms borrowed from physics, acoustics and mathematics. Even the 'unscientific' aleatoric element in Stockhausen's music he claims to have derived directly from studies of statistics, random structures, the aleatory behaviour of noise structures and other scientific disciplines in Professor Werner Meyer-Eppler's seminars. This gentleman, with whom Stockhausen studied communication theory and phonetics at Bonn University from 1954 to 1956, and who was a trained physicist and phoneticist, gave the movement one sort of extra-musical stimulus and terminology; the electronic studio technician gave it another. Both influences can be clearly seen in the inaugural number of *Die Reihe* (1955) on Electronic Music. It is the international mouthpiece of the movement, and is edited by Herbert Eimert, who was the founder of the new Cologne Electronic Studio, and Stockhausen himself.

Perhaps the war finally dashed, for this generation, any lingering hope that musical structure could continue to play second fiddle to fine emotions in the making of a piece. Schoenberg had already paved the way by writing music more structure-conscious than any since Bach and the Viennese classics, Berg had used rhythmic systems and extra-musical numerologies, and Webern wrote some of the first music in which the musical idea, as Alexander Goehr would say, *is* the process employed – as opposed to its being a statement that arises *within* the process. The status of technology and rationality was high, 'irrational' was a dirty word, and composers saw the imposition of externally-conceived patterns on to music as something not only *new* (previous composers having been too fearful of the 'paper-music!' accusation), but *permissible* in aesthetic society.

2
Kreuzspiel

Such was the world into which the twenty-three-year-old Stockhausen graduated from the Cologne High School for Music in 1951. He was born in Mödrath bei Köln on the 22nd of August 1928. His parents came from humble families. Stockhausen's mother died in 1941; she had been in a sanatorium since 1933. His father, who fought in the war from 1939 on, was killed in Hungary.* Stockhausen's father was a village schoolmaster, the first 'intellectual' in a traditionally 'peasant' family of farmers. This meant that he was obliged to collect party contributions (*Winterhilfe* etc.) and was directly answerable to the Gestapo. Being a teacher, he was constantly ordered from one village to another, though from the age of five to the outbreak of the war, Stockhausen enjoyed a relative stability of domicile. From ten to twelve he was at an *Oberschule* (grammar school, more or less), then at a state boarding school. For this latter, requirements were very stringent, not simply in respect of intelligence and physical health, but also (of course) in terms of racial purity. To this end, Stockhausen's father had been to the trouble of tracing the family's roots back to the Thirty Years War (all farmers), and had done the same for his wife's family tree (though she was in the sanatorium by this time). The discipline in this school was extremely militaristic – the concept of private leisure and activity hardly existed. So, for example, a day began with everyone rising to the call of a trumpet at six o'clock, then there were sports, and then a meeting in the square to hear ideologically-slanted information about the war (all this before breakfast). Having learnt English and Latin at his previous school, Stockhausen was put in a class where many of the pupils were two or three years older than he was. The result of this was that in 1944 the vast majority of his class became soldiers, but Stockhausen, being still too young, was sent to various youth camps (to help build the Western Wall against the allied forces). After that he served in a *Kriegslazarett* (military hospital), taking care of the wounded (including English and American soldiers – he was probably the only person in the hospital to have studied English) for about six months. This didn't, he says, make him a pacifist – his attitude was 'if fighting has to be done, it has to be done', not so much for the gain of a political faction, but to preserve one's own home (by the time he came to the front, Germany was well on the way to losing the war, of course). Generally speaking, though,

---

* Karl Wörner, *Stockhausen: Life and Work*, Faber, London, 1973.

his experience in the hospital of meeting soldiers of different races tended to convince him of the similarity of different nationalities rather than the difference, and of the complete impersonality that overtakes any large group of people. (Thus were the seeds of *Hymnen* sown.)

Stockhausen learnt the piano from the age of six, and later the violin and oboe too. In 1947 he began his piano studies at the Cologne Music School. Simultaneously he began to study musicology and philosophy at the University of Cologne. To maintain himself he played the piano for jazz groups, and (this the musicologists of the future will love) even became an improvising accompanist for a magician. He had about five two-hour lessons with Frank Martin in 1950, by which time he had a good knowledge of Bartók, Stravinsky and Schoenberg. He had written a dissertation of over a hundred pages on Bartók's Sonata for Two Pianos and Percussion, which already shows the tendency to think in terms of parameters or dimensions one at a time, separated rather than inseparable parts of something; and he is already concerned with conflicts of structure between them. Deliberations on this problem have been central to his composing ever since. Bartók's experiments with the contacts between piano and percussion sonorities were to bear fruit later in Stockhausen's *Kontakte*. He had also composed as a student *Choral*, *Chöre für Doris*, *Drei Lieder* for alto and chamber orchestra, *Formel* for orchestra, *Sonatine* for violin and piano, *Drei Chöre*, etc. – and became a competent pianist, and, as already mentioned, jazz pianist.

But 1951 marks not only this graduation from a college education that had deadened the musical past for him, as he has said, it also marks his first encounter with Messiaen's piano piece *Mode de valeurs et d'intensités* (1949) on a gramophone record which he heard at Darmstadt that summer. This tough, tightly-knit piece, something of an isolated work in Messiaen's *oeuvre*, had an amazing effect on Stockhausen. His previous violin sonatina had been conventional, simple serialism with touches of Schoenberg and Martin visible – singing phrases and cheeky rhythms. Then, under the influence of Messiaen's piece, that autumn he wrote *Kreuzspiel* which inhabits a different world and represents a violently clean severing of the umbilical cord. He had meanwhile decided to travel in January 1952 to Paris to attend Messiaen's course on aesthetics and analysis at the Conservatoire to which he went twice a week for about a year. Messiaen analysed Mozart's piano concertos, Gregorian chant and Indian music from a rhythmic point of view, also the early Netherlanders, Debussy, Webern, Stravinsky, and his own music from first sketches to finished article. Following Messiaen's example Stockhausen learnt (he tells us) to transform what he had previously dismissed as dead music into a living inner experience, productive of new music. 'Man is only a vessel' as Webern said; and Messiaen's book *The Technique of my Musical Language* clearly indicates Messiaen's self-confessed eclecticism, a thing which really shows up in Stockhausen more clearly in much later works like *Telemusik*, *Hymnen* and *Stockhoven – Beethausen Opus 1970*, a recorded version of *Kurzwellen* based on the music of Beethoven.

In Stockhausen's works of this period there is, however, an almost total rejection of our

European past. The only influences detectable in *Kreuzspiel*, for instance, are Messiaen, Indian music (suggested by high drum pattering, a pointillistic piece by the fellow Darmstadt student Goeyvarts – Sonata for 2 Pianos whose middle movements also cross registers, and just a sniff of Webern in the purity and austerity of texture (he knew only Webern's Five Movements for String Quartet Op. 5). Let us now look at this work as a representative of the first period of Stockhausen's career.

The novelty which so struck Stockhausen about Messiaen's piano piece was that it boldly formalised *four* parameters or dimensions of the music. Things normally left to good taste and fine feelings, such as dynamics, were no longer emotionally determined, but formally determined; and, what's more, separately determined. In introducing his piece, Messiaen wrote, 'Ce morceau utilise un mode de hauteurs (36 sons), de valeurs (24 durées), d'attaques (12 attaques), et d'intensités (7 nuances). Il est entièrement écrit dans le mode.' Substitute, as Stockhausen says, 'series' for 'mode' and you have something very close to total serialism, a method of musical thinking which has influenced Stockhausen ever since.

Kreuzspiel, which is scored for oboe, bass clarinet, piano and three percussion, is the first example of it. The first performance (Darmstadt 1952) was accompanied by the scandal customary with most of Stockhausen's premières. It is, like the other works of the period – *Spiel* for orchestra, *Schlagquartett* for pianist and three timpanists, *Punkte* for orchestra (first version) and the first version of *Kontra-Punkte* – pointillistic in the sense that each note, duration and dynamic follows an overall separate set of instructions, is *individually* organised, as opposed to its being a lesser or greater *member* of some hierarchy which is dominated by some 'goal'. It does not mean that one hears lots of 'single notes' any more than one does in Webern, but the texture in both cases is comparatively spare.

It is in three sections. 'Crossplay', as the title may be translated, occurs in several ways. Example 1 shows how, during twelve twelve-note sets, the pitches are permutated across to make the final set's first hexachord resemble the first set's second hexachord, and vice versa. The numbered curves show another, dyadic, way of looking at the 'crossplay'.* The piano only plays very high or very low, the medium high register belongs to the oboe, the medium low to the bass clarinet. The number of notes in each of these registers is written by the side of each set. The medium registers have more and more of the notes to the half-way point, then less and less. The positioning of the notes in either the high registers or the low registers is also subject to 'crossplay' for the six which were high in the first set have gradually become the six that are low in the final set, and vice versa. This is a result of a set (7254361) which rotates pitches through the seven octaves.

Just as Messiaen coupled pitches and durations together, so Stockhausen here attaches a duration between 1 and 12 to each pitch class, consequently they are permutated along

* *Kreuzspiel* was by no means the first to use this type of rotation. See, for instance, Krenek's 'Lamentatio Jeremiae Prophetae' (1941), discussed in *Problems of Modern Music*, ed. P. H. Lang, W. W. Norton and Co., New York, 1962.

Ex. 1

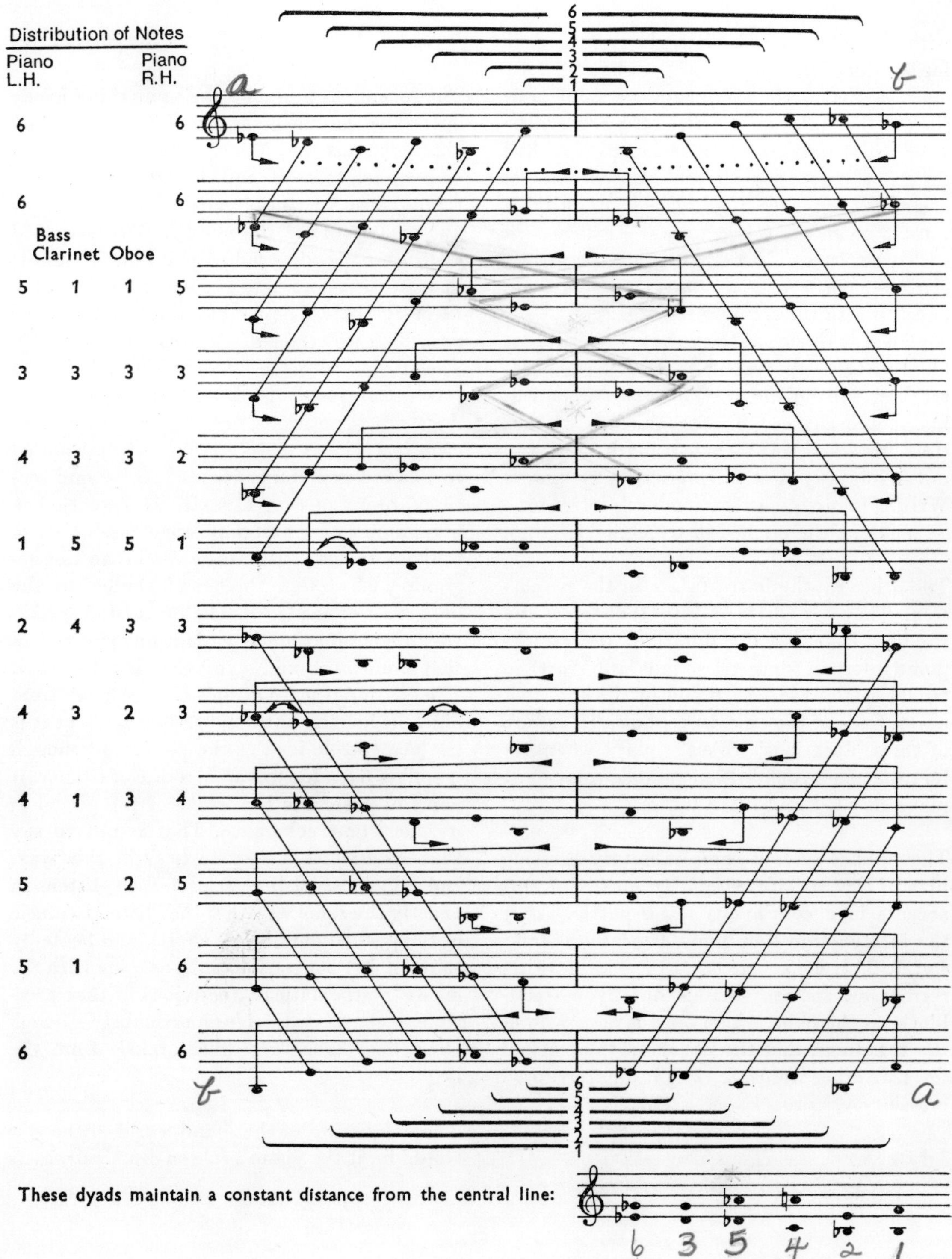

These dyads maintain a constant distance from the central line:

with the pitches. Indeed, a closer precedent for the duration scheme seems to be *Les Yeux dans les Roues*, the sixth movement of Messiaen's *Livre d'Orgue* (1951), rather than the *Étude*. The organ piece attaches pitches and durations together again and also permutates a straight sequence of durations-cum-pitches 1 to 12 in the following manner – *extrêmes au centre*, *extrêmes au centre retrograde*, *centre aux extrêmes*, *centre aux extrêmes retrograde*, and ends up with the retrograde sequence 12 to 1. A glance at Example 2 will show the closeness of Stockhausen's system to the work of his teacher, written the previous year, though it had not been seen by Stockhausen at that time. Messiaen was father to mathematics in music in a way that the more usually quoted Webern (more obviously 'modern') never was. So much for the pitched instruments' rhythm.

The other rhythmic strata are in the percussion. They are divided into tom-toms and tumbas. Here are the durations (or attack-point intervals since all sounds are short) in triplet semiquavers as found in the tom-tom parts. Each of the four drums has a repertoire of three 'durations' which it plays whenever its turn comes round. For example, tom-tom 1 plays only 1, 4 and 7 (see Ex. 2).

The tumbas have a complementary crossing plan. They articulate sets by means of soft accents in a continuous finger-patter. After the introduction they move from the regular set: 1, 2, 3, 4, 5, 6/7, 8, 9, 10, 11, 12 to its retrograde, specially struck out by a woodblock, at the point where set 6 is occurring in the tom-toms, and then back to the original form. In other words, a straight uninterrupted crossing-over process.

The second section does the same thing inside out. The middle registers (oboe and bass clarinet) start and finish, using material that comes back to itself, and the extreme registers (piano) are what the music moves towards and away from in the middle. Widely-spaced chords are used instead of 'pointillistic' simple lines in the piano, and the percussionists play three cymbals. The final section combines the preceding processes in a rather complex way. The piano and wind proceed through the 12 sets (Example 1) backwards with the same registral dispositions and the same notes in each instrument as in section one; but added to this is a superimposition of the second section around a central axis. This reaches a maximum point half way, then fades out, so that we are left with music similar to the beginning of section three and similar to the beginning of the work. The percussion is likewise a combination of sections one and two in that tom-toms and cymbals play together. The continual sense of slow change away from a musical shape until one arrives back at it is the perceptible idea of the piece, and though it suffers from too unvaried a rate of change, it gains over some other works of the period in its consistent coherence. That is not to say that *Kreuzspiel* is *easy* to hear in this way. Indeed, most listeners prefer to listen in exactly the same way that they listen to music of the past (it entails less effort), and heatedly to resist any suggestions such as mine with the insult 'mathematical!', oblivious of that principle – mathematical proportioning – which alone has made their music music from the beginning.

The uniqueness of the sound world – who else would limit the piano's role so drastically? – is

Ex. 2

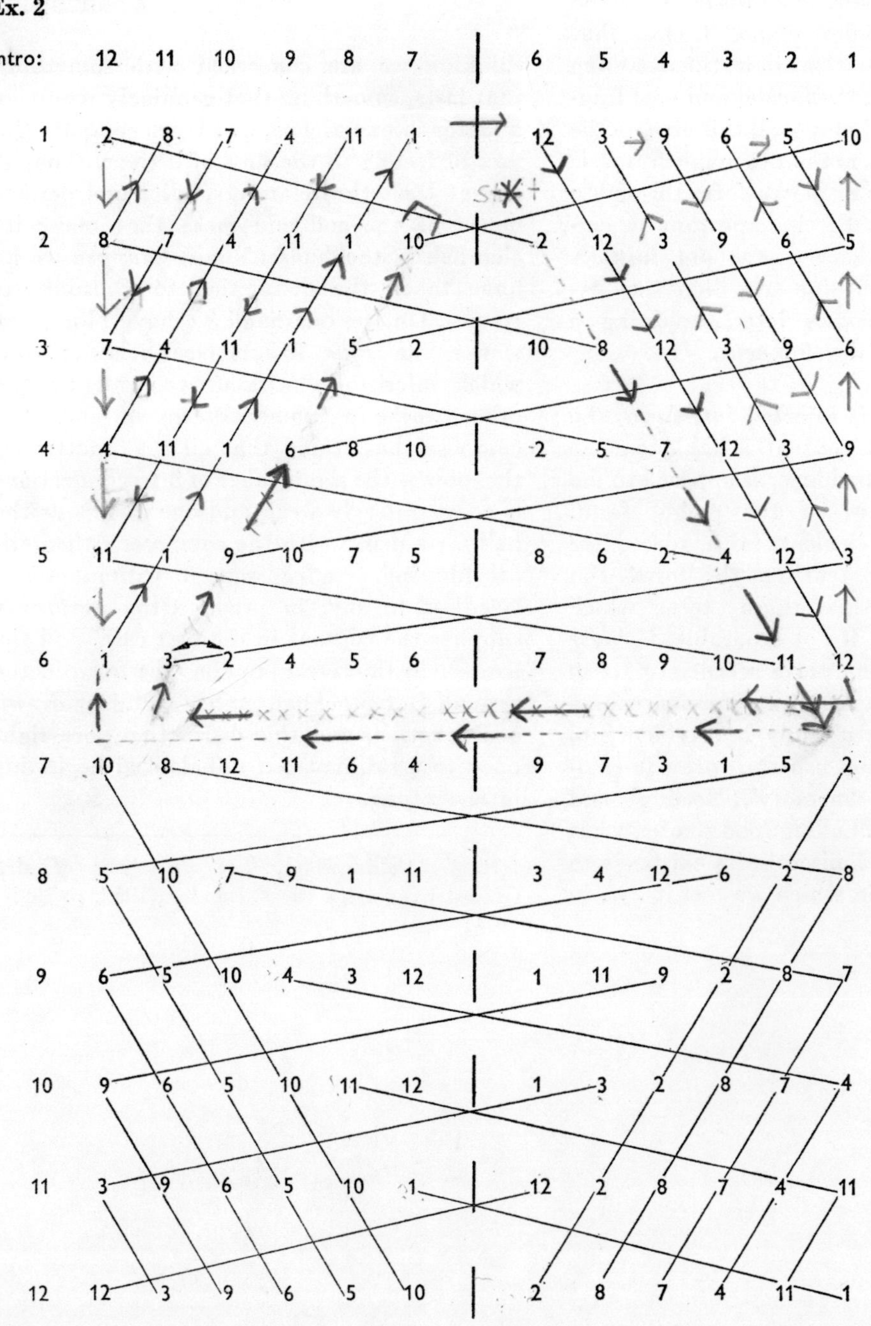
Intro: 12 11 10 9 8 7 6 5 4 3 2 1
1 2 8 7 4 11 1 12 3 9 6 5 10
2 8 7 4 11 1 10 2 12 3 9 6 5
3 7 4 11 1 5 2 10 8 12 3 9 6
4 4 11 1 6 8 10 2 5 7 12 3 9
5 11 1 9 10 7 5 8 6 2 4 12 3
6 1 3 2 4 5 6 7 8 9 10 11 12
7 10 8 12 11 6 4 9 7 3 1 5 2
8 5 10 7 9 1 11 3 4 12 6 2 8
9 6 5 10 4 3 12 1 11 9 2 8 7
10 9 6 5 10 11 12 1 3 2 8 7 4
11 3 9 6 5 10 1 12 2 8 7 4 11
12 12 3 9 6 5 10 2 8 7 4 11 1

typical of Stockhausen. The tom-toms, placed either side of the lidless piano, so close that they invoke reverberations in it, the pattering tumbas at the back, the formal and cool fragments that the wind play – all this creates the impression of a work not out to make dramatic gestures, but out to display a form through a chosen medium. And it is important to emphasise that Stockhausen was not *initially* concerned with youthful and dionysiac expressionism; this comes later, reversing a common pattern of development.

However, if music is injected *into* form, the moment-to-moment 'content' is liable to come up with some curious things, as opposed to the logic and coherence of the global form. The uncontrolled element in a piece like *Kreuzspiel* is the 'content' not the 'form'. I'm availing myself of these thorny terms which are distinguishable, if not separable, because some such distinction plays a crucial part in Stockhausen's thought. Our experience of a piece of music can usefully be divided into 'being' and 'knowing' aspects, 'present emotional state' and 'memory', 'feeling' and 'thinking'. As R. G. Collingwood wrote: 'what we feel is certainly limited in its existence to the here and now in which we feel it . . . in thinking we are concerned with something that lasts, something that genuinely recurs as a factor in experience. . . . If we compare the flux of feeling to the flow of a river, thought has at least the relative solidity and permanence of the soil and rocks that make its channel.'* Stockhausen's post-*Gruppen* works have taken the distinction to unusual extremes. On the one hand we have blue-print works like *Plus Minus* (see below p. 93) which offer form without content, on the other, works in 'moment' form, of which the composer has stated that all that matters is the 'now' – the significance of interconnections is comparatively weak and one can leave the hall for a drink with the composer's theoretical blessing – offer content without form. Needless to say, in practice the performer supplies the content in the first case, and the listener instinctively supplies the form in the second. But Stockhausen has certainly drawn a distinction, and this distinction goes right back to a brilliant but unbalanced beginning in *Kreuzspiel*.

---

* R. G. Collingwood, *The Principles of Art*, Oxford University Press, London, 1958, p. 159.

3

Kontra-Punkte, Piano Pieces I-IV Electronic Studies

The next phase of Stockhausen's career, 1952–3, consists of three works, *Kontra-Punkte*, *Piano Pieces I–IV* and *Electronic Study 1*, and has elements of both 'pointillistic' style and 'group' style.

Nr. 1 *Kontra-Punkte* for ten instruments was the first work that Stockhausen felt to be fully mature, hence the 'Nr. 1' affixed to the title. It was written in 1952 and first performed in Cologne in 1953. *Kontra-Punkte* means both 'counterpoints' and 'against *Punkte*', in other words it is simultaneously a new piece and a methodological repudiation of the difficulties posed by his earlier piece *Punkte* for orchestra (unrevised version), or indeed by all 'pointillistic' works. In *Punkte* (as in *Kreuzspiel*) single notes and single rhythmic attacks were the units which were systematically organised, giving rise to the law of diminishing returns operative in a texture which is too consistently varied.*

In *Kontra-Punkte* the unit of organisation is not just the single note, but includes many other factors such as elaborate strings of notes, big chords, real 'groups' and lengthy tempo-defined sections. In short, what is perceived as a unit becomes larger and more like what is normally understood to be a musical idea – several components making up one entity of unified character. It was not first conceived thus, however. The first version was much more monochrome, more 'pointillistic'; he rewrote it very soon afterwards, adding the melismata etc. that we know.

There are 46 sections, each with a different tempo mark. These latter are selected from a tempo scale of seven steps: ♪=120, 126, 136, 152, 168, 184 and 200. This foreshadows the later *serial* use of a tempo scale. Here the first tempo is used much more than any of the others, which is contrary to the serial principles of the later works, though the whole question of the audibility of such schemes is a vexed one. To return to more realistic ground, the ten instruments are chosen so that they may be grouped according to timbral similarity into six groups: 1. flute/bassoon, 2. clarinet/bass-clarinet, 3. trumpet/trombone, 4. violin/cello, 5. piano, 6. harp. Or alternatively into two groups if separated into wind-produced sound and string-produced sound.

* In the little-known orchestral work *Formel* written immediately after *Kreuzspiel*, Stockhausen had already made an attempt to move away from the problems of pointillism by using twelve motives or configurations as opposed to single notes.

One of the most important ideas of the work is that the instruments gradually drop out, finally leaving only one sonority, the piano's. The sequence of dropping out (a large scale 'release' plan, as when the notes of a chord are released one after the other) is as follows:

1 Trumpet
2 Trombone
3 Bassoon
4 Violin
5 Bass-clarinet
6 Harp
7 Clarinet
8 Cello
9 Flute
10 Piano

The rate at which the dropping out occurs follows the curved lines of the above plan at a consistent relative ratio of approximately 11 : 4. That is to say, the interval of time in beats between the finish of the bassoon part and the finish of the violin part is rather less than three times (11 : 4) the interval between the finish of the cello part and the finish of the flute part. The same applies to the violin/bass-clarinet finishing interval and the clarinet/cello finishing interval; also to the bass-clarinet/harp one and the harp/clarinet one; also to the 'outer' system – trombone/harp and harp/piano. In each case the large time interval is first, so that in general the instruments drop out slowly at first, then more and more quickly; and this general tendency is systematically shaped by factors depending on the tone-colour that is dropping out. It is another example of Stockhausen's careful attention to dimensions of form not normally systematised.

Chapter Three

Just as the timbres become more limited to the end so do the dynamics and note values. The seven* dynamics tend statistically towards *pp* as all other markings drop out and the note values become comparatively even and restful. Thus the work moves into something nearer the future style – it becomes increasingly *kontra* the principles of *Punkte*.

Although composed at the same time as *Piano Pieces I–IV*, it has more in common with both *Piano Piece V* of a year later, with its rich Germanic chords in the piano and its consistent textures; and also with *Zeitmasze*† of two years later, with its abundant and complex instrumental melismata set off against long sustained notes. *Kontra-Punkte's* melismata, with their leanings towards the aperiodical and their wide leaps, now repeating fixed static pitches, now forging strongly ahead into new territory, have an exultant dionysiac quality such as could only spring from an unusually intense creative joy.

Of the projected cycle of twenty-one piano pieces, Stockhausen has so far (1971) composed eleven. They are, he says, his drawings, in which he is necessarily excluded from the world of colour modulation – indeed there is no string stopping or framework hitting either – he is obliged to rely on pure shaping of the eighty-eight monochrome pitches.

Piano Pieces III and *II* were written in 1952 for Doris, who was then his wife, and *Pieces I* and *IV* were subsequently added in 1953 to make a set with the designation *Nr. 2*, which

* Not six, as Stockhausen says in *Texte* II, p. 20.
† Sometimes spelled *Zeitmasse*.

is usually played as such, and was the nearest Stockhausen had ever got to writing a work in many separate movements, until the recent *Herbstmusik*. The entire set is dedicated to its first performer, Marcelle Mercenier.

The first piece is composed of ever-alternating chromatic hexachords, all the notes from C up to F alternating with those from F sharp up to B. The ordering within these two collections varies widely following certain subcollection ideas, and if the reader considers the number of possibilities when one takes in, in addition to the single-note orderings, the possible range of simultaneities, from two part to six part, which can be placed anywhere within the collection, then the apparent limitations of such a repetitive scheme dissolve. There are occasionally bigger chords too which borrow from the neighbouring hexachord. One such is a nine-note chord (bar 11) in which the fingers must differentiate five separate dynamic levels. The notes are attacked together and released successively, articulating, or at least following, a subcollection idea which moves across the hexachords. Stockhausen makes the point about this process, that it mirrors bar 1 in which there are successive attacks (or arpeggiations of chords) which are released together by lifting the sustaining pedal. Berg presented a similar mirror pattern at the beginning and end of the third *Altenberg Lied* in which a twelve-note chord is attacked in a block at the beginning and then slowly released in a certain order, and the same chord is at the end successively attacked in the same order and then released as a block. As so often with forms-projected-into-music, the Second Viennese School were the first; their mentality, like that of the Darmstadt School, was very structure-conscious, only they were in touch with Beethoven and the Darmstadt School was not.

Stockhausen wrote an article on the first twelve groups of this piece after doing some analysis of Webern's music. It is the only one of the four in which there are articulative 'pauses' in sufficient quantity to justify a discussion in terms of 'groups', and Stockhausen regarded it therefore as a step forward. The piece was written, he tells us, in two days, with the help of 'some measurements and proportionings'. But only after he'd composed the piece and after the analysis experience did he see in it the relationships between the groups that he had composed quickly and intuitively, with 'some measurements'. So far, it would seem we have a background system ('measurements') behind a complex foreground in which the frenzy of creation unconsciously made certain satisfying symmetries. But when one examines what, in Stockhausen's opinion, constitutes a correspondence or close relationship one begins to think that in places the analysis is more wishful thinking than reality. In order to make a macrocosmic representation of a hexachord by 'groups', he divides the piece up into macrogroups of six groups each, in which each separate group corresponds to an 'opposite number' group in another macrogroup, but, as with the pitch hexachords, the order is shuffled. He defines the relationships by dynamic, rhythmic, chordal, contour and durational (1–6 quavers) factors, but these factors are so irregularly articulated in many groups that other intergroup correspondences are equally possible. For example, group seven (bar eight) has much more in common with group four (bar four) than with the group Stockhausen suggests, group six.

It is a very complex piece—two sets interact to produce a different tempo-ratio for each group, but the complexity arises from very widely differentiated *short* events constantly changing, even within groups. The most satisfactory type of musical complexity is offered not by music in which there are many *items*, but by music in which there are many *arguments*. Stockhausen came to realise this shortly afterwards; he wrote: 'a constant succession of contrasts becomes just as "boring" as constant repetition: we stop expecting anything specific, and cannot be surprised: the overall impression of a succession of contrasts is levelled down to a single information'.* But, of course, this piece is short enough to achieve a certain splendour of *élan* despite all, and it is interesting that Stockhausen seems to miss the point of his own piece. At any rate, Stockhausen later avoids this type of structure in favour of larger formations more closely resembling those which he tries to fit on to this piece. His awareness of the information theory type of aesthetics becomes more and more prominent in his music until it eventually, at certain points, *becomes* the music, as I will show later. And the beginnings can first be seen clearly in his article on Webern ('Structure and Experiential Time') quoted above, and in the misguided analytical application of it to *Piano Piece I*, which misguidedness simply shows how radically his thinking was changing during his course with Meyer-Eppler at Bonn University.

* K. Stockhausen, 'Structure and Experiential Time', *Die Reihe*, vol. 2, p. 64.

The other pieces of the set are rather shorter, and as they are all to be played 'as fast as possible' they share the general character of brilliance and quick contrasts with the first one. Likewise they all have a fairly realistic pitch background which very complex rhythms and widely spaced registral dispositions deliberately obfuscate. *Piano Piece II* is built on two trichords

Ex. 3

which are reordered, transposed and in the middle elaborately permutated; *III* is built on a five-note collection

Ex. 4

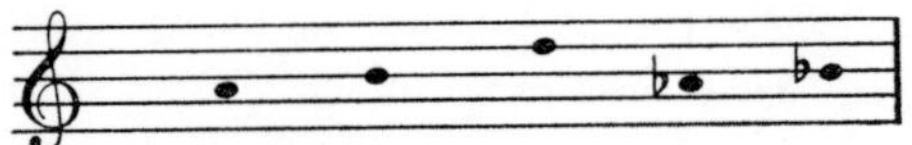

and *IV* on the trichord

Ex. 5

This latter piece is a study in two part counterpoint in which both parts retain their identity by means of one dimension alone, that of dynamic marking. The listener can follow a string of, for instance, five *forte* notes, whilst the register changes from bottom to top, long silences separate the notes, other, nearer notes of the second voice intervene and the trichordal germ (see example above) runs *across* the two voices; in other words, there is much to counter the following of this *forte* line and tempt the ear away, but the joy of the piece is that one learns to yield to temptation and to resist it at the same time, and so to appreciate the several levels simultaneously.

To show how the pitch structure of this early period tends to work, and how similar it often is to the cellular thinking and contour-consciousness of pre-serial Webern, here is the shortest piece, number *III*, followed by an analysis of the voice part of Webern's *Funf Geistliche Lieder*, op. 15, no. 1 (see Exx. 6 and 7).

At this same time, Stockhausen composed his first electronic music. He had, however, already composed a piece of *musique concrète*, *Étude* (1952), which was the fruit of his year in Paris and was realised at the studio of the French Radio. The Paris *musique concrète* group, after the example of Varèse, was concerned with the transformation or distortion of already recorded sounds. Analysis of these sounds with oscillographs and filters was an important part of Stockhausen's activity there – he spent much time analysing reverberated and unreverberated percussion sounds, speech and noises of all sorts. He there began his immersion in sound as such, making tape loops of single sounds and playing them back for days on end.

Studie 1, Nr. 3/i and *Studie 2*, Nr. 3/ii were composed in 1953 and 1954 respectively. No doubt Stockhausen, having gleaned some experience in Paris, returned to the new and more flexible studio Herbert Eimert had just established in Cologne with considerable enthusiasm. *Studie 1* only consists of entirely pure sine tones (it was the first piece to use them, Stockhausen tells us) and has an extremely limited array of pitches – a 'drawing' for later electronic works. The limitation of intervals to major thirds, minor sixths and minor tenths makes for a rather monotonous piece. It is a case of elaborate systematisation being used to achieve something that fantasy could have done much better in half the time. Like Messiaen's *Mode de valeurs et d'intensités* it uses fixed proportions – in this case, the lower the pitch the shorter it is, calculated by multiplying the frequency by $\frac{1}{10}$ and making the resulting number equal the centimetres of tape used for that note – and serial dynamics moving by steps of 4 db within a six-element series, having first equalised all frequencies by feeding in an audio-response curve. It also interestingly foreshadows the procedures of *Gruppen* (see below pp. 62–63) in its use of ratios to generate a string of notes (or tempi and durations in *Gruppen*):

12 : 5   8 : 5   5 : 4
4 : 5   5 : 12

which six-part progression generates foreground, middleground and background – a string of six notes, the starting points of six strings and the starting points of six blocks-of-strings! Thus it is a strict example of total serialisation.

Much more interesting formally, though timbrally it is also very circumscribed, is *Studie 2*. It is characteristic of Stockhausen that he selects quite a constricted range of material, then proceeds to cover it totally, to use up *all* the possibilities that imagination considers worth while, just as in his later works a limited sound world dominates for a long passage of time or for the entire piece – in *Refrain*, for example, which is for Piano, Celesta, Vibraphone and light percussion. His material in

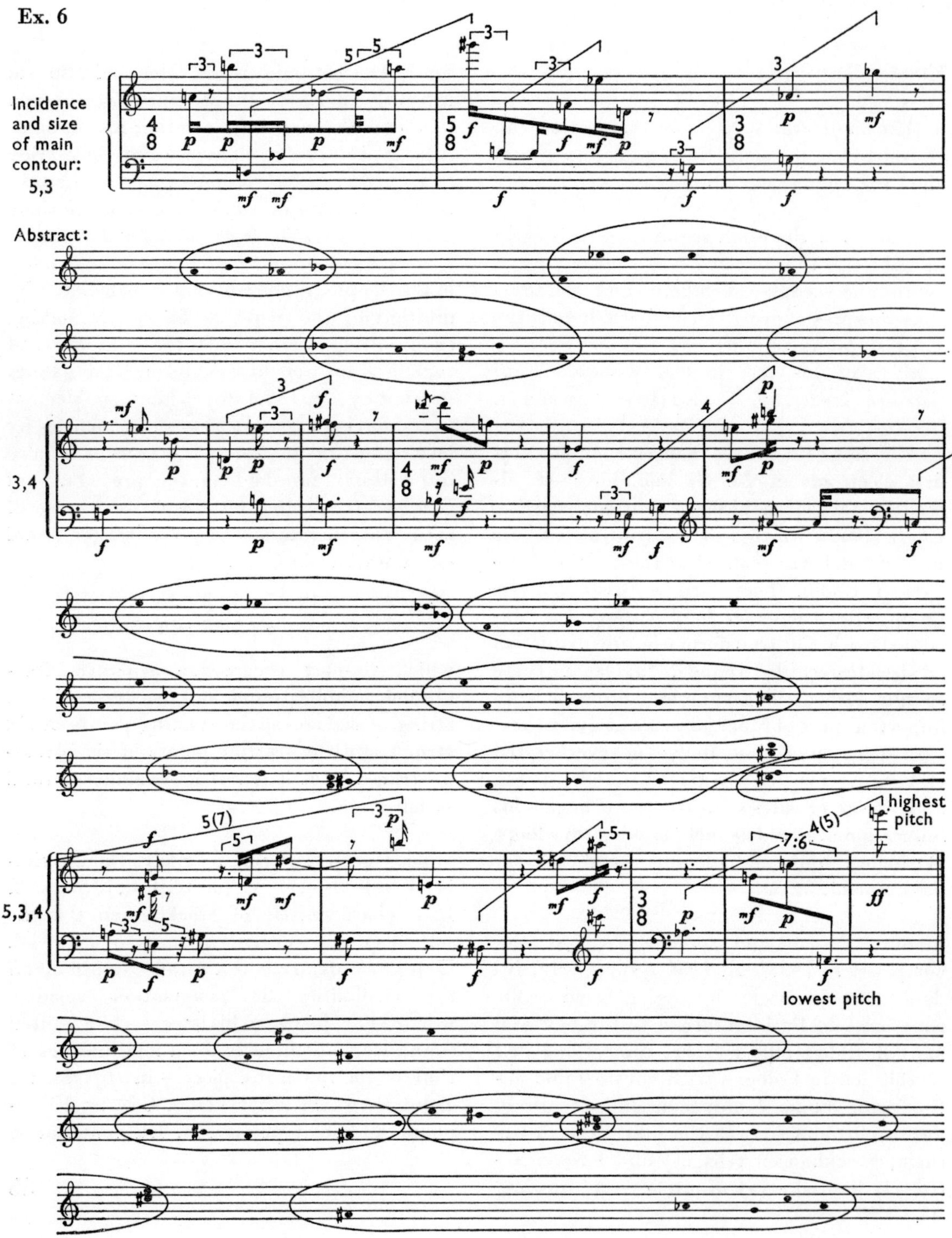
Ex. 6
Incidence and size of main contour: 5,3
Abstract:
3,4
5,3,4
highest pitch
lowest pitch

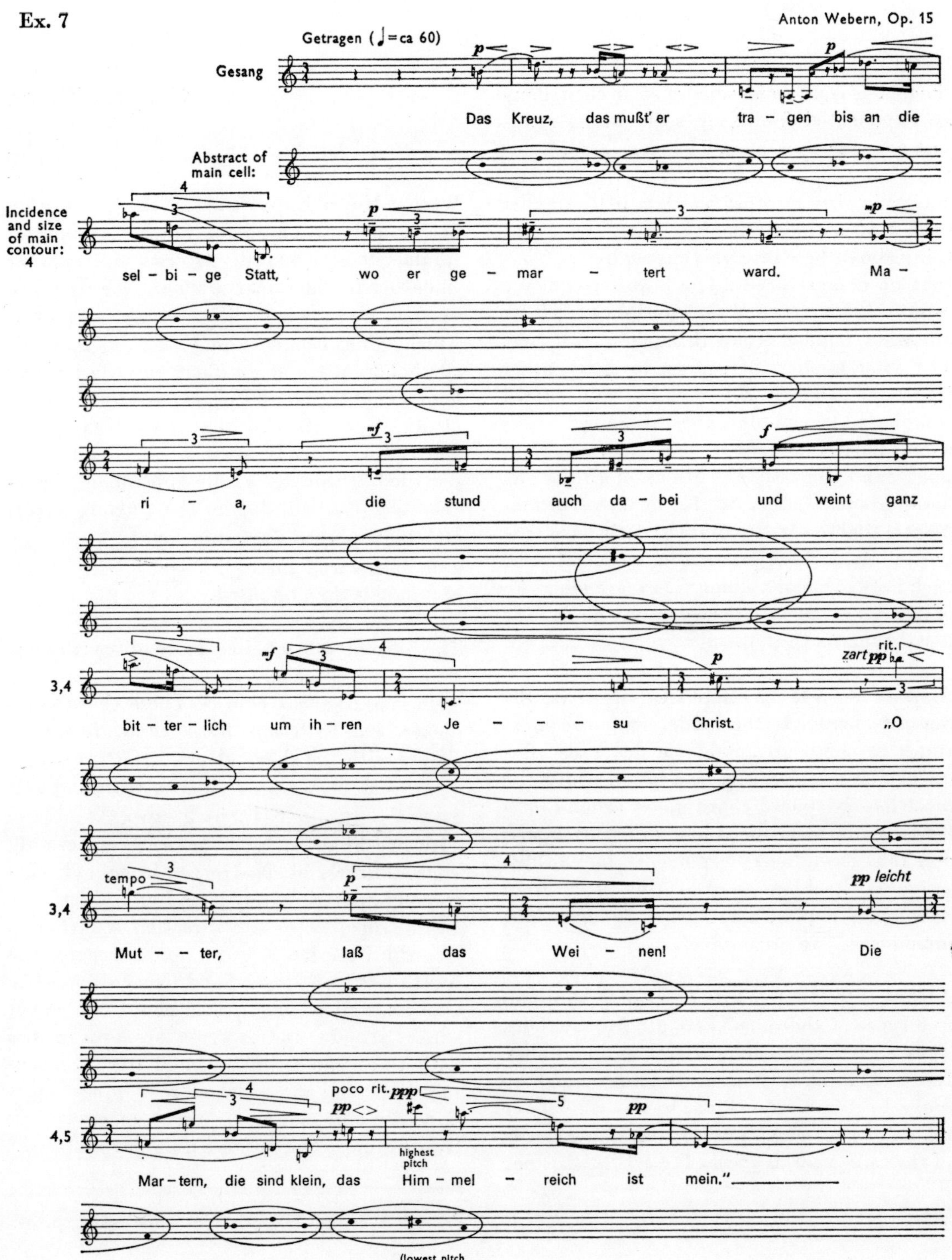
Ex. 7
Anton Webern, Op. 15
Getragen (♩=ca 60)
Gesang
Das Kreuz, das mußt' er tra – gen bis an die
Abstract of main cell:
Incidence and size of main contour: 4
sel – bi – ge Statt, wo er ge – mar – tert ward. Ma –
ri – a, die stund auch da – bei und weint ganz
3,4
bit – ter – lich um ih – ren Je – – – – su Christ. „O
rit.
zart
tempo
3,4
Mut – – ter, laß das Wei – nen! Die
pp leicht
poco rit.
4,5
Mar – tern, die sind klein, das Him – mel – reich ist mein."
highest pitch
(lowest pitch in Bass Clarinet)

Studie 2 is eighty-one sine tones pitched along an exponential frequency scale which spans just over seven octaves. The steps are all perceived as equal and are a little over $\frac{1}{10}$ of an octave in size, in other words a little smaller than $\frac{3}{4}$ of a whole tone. The most significant thing about these intervals chosen by $\sqrt[25]{5}$ is that no octaves occur. The lowest frequency used is 100 c.p.s., and no multiple of 100 by any whole number occurs throughout the scale. The same applies, of course, to every other frequency. Thus Stockhausen has constructed completely logical 'unnatural' material as far as our harmonic series is concerned. The tingling sound is partly the result of combining non-harmonic intervals. He replaces instrumental timbre with its characteristic harmonic partials with five-part non-harmonic chords, each note of equal volume. They are made up of the sine tones, either densely packed or loosely spaced (Ex. 8).

Another formal characteristic is that the densest chord has the ladder with the most rungs to climb up and down on (every frequency on the scale can be a base), whilst the most loosely spaced chord glides around on a ladder with rungs about half an octave apart, and thus has a 'near-harmonious' lack of dissonance. Stockhausen uses this scale from dissonance approaching 'noise' to 'near-harmoniousness' to great effect.

Just as there are five sine tones per chord and five types of chord, so there are five sections. They each have a strong character and, unlike those of previous works, are long enough to make a distinct impression. In this way above all, this work, which was written in the spring of the same year as *Piano Piece V*, strikes one as a model for the next period and the beginning of Stockhausen's contact with Professor Werner Meyer-Eppler's ideas. The first section has a melodic character in that strings of similar density chords succeed one another smoothly in the linear manner. The dynamic norm is against which things occur. I should explain that this symbol from the score illustrates the relative loudness of the chord (height) and by the angle of its slopes its rise time and decay time. There is no 'steady state' – all sounds were recorded through a diminuendoing echo-chamber (contributing to the tingling effect) and then played forwards for and backwards for . An exact envelope is then imposed.

The second section has more discontinuous shapes and especially thick densities resulting from simultaneous chords. These chord complexes are built up by several 'forwards' shapes with the sharp attack or several 'backwards' shapes with the soft attack in a row. As always with Stockhausen, 'what is like becomes only approximately like; correspondences only correspond approximately',* and an insignificant gesture in an opposite direction is included. The third section is quick and staccato, the fourth has long sounds, and hence dream-like rhythm, and widely spaced chord complexes whose attacks and releases are arpeggiated with the utmost fantasy, and the fifth contains all the above types in a much more unpredictable manner, as a rearrangement and transformation of by now familiar material.

* 'Structure and Experiential Time', *ibid.*, p. 74.

Ex. 8

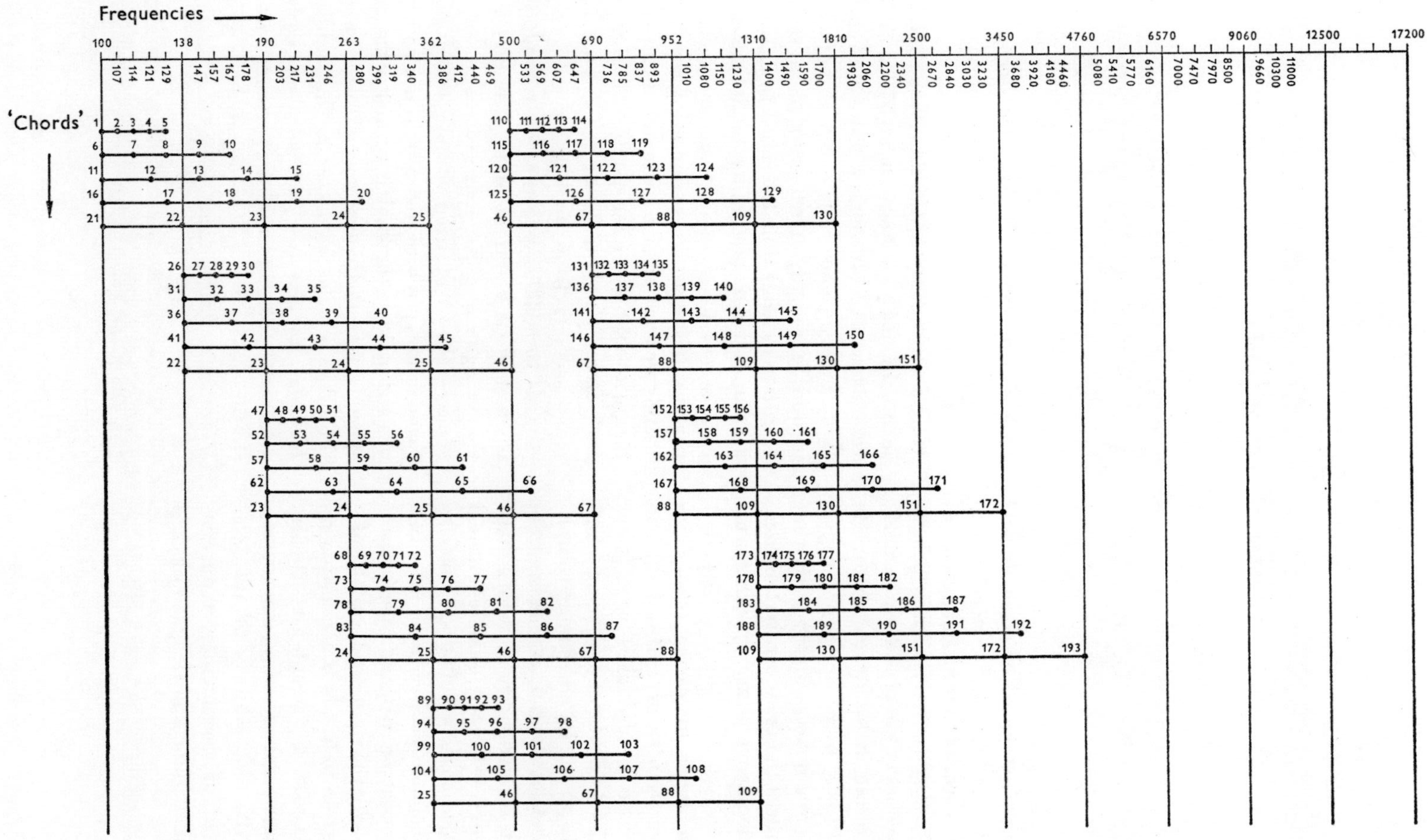

Frequencies →

100 107 114 121 129 138 147 157 167 178 190 203 217 231 246 263 280 299 319 340 362 386 412 440 469 500 533 569 607 647 690 736 785 837 893 952 1010 1080 1150 1230 1310 1400 1490 1590 1700 1810 1930 2060 2200 2340 2500 2670 2840 3030 3230 3450 3680 3920 4180 4460 4760 5080 5410 5770 6160 6570 7000 7470 7970 8500 9060 9660 10300 11000 12500 17200

'Chords' ↓

1 2 3 4 5
6 7 8 9 10
11 12 13 14 15
16 17 18 19 20
21 22 23 24 25

26 27 28 29 30
31 32 33 34 35
36 37 38 39 40
41 42 43 44 45
22 23 24 25 46

47 48 49 50 51
52 53 54 55 56
57 58 59 60 61
62 63 64 65 66
23 24 25 46 67

68 69 70 71 72
73 74 75 76 77
78 79 80 81 82
83 84 85 86 87
24 25 46 67 88

89 90 91 92 93
94 95 96 97 98
99 100 101 102 103
104 105 106 107 108
25 46 67 88 109

110 111 112 113 114
115 116 117 118 119
120 121 122 123 124
125 126 127 128 129
46 67 88 109 130

131 132 133 134 135
136 137 138 139 140
141 142 143 144 145
146 147 148 149 150
67 88 109 130 151

152 153 154 155 156
157 158 159 160 161
162 163 164 165 166
167 168 169 170 171
88 109 130 151 172

173 174 175 176 177
178 179 180 181 182
183 184 185 186 187
188 189 190 191 192
109 130 151 172 193

4

New Theories

Before going any further in the chronological discussion of the works, it will be necessary to explain the new theories that Stockhausen was hatching at about this time, with which he wrote the next series of works and which mark, again, a new phase in his development. He started his studies with Professor Meyer-Eppler in 1954, and it seems highly likely that this gentleman was the main catalyst of these radical developments in Stockhausen's thought, not only in the 'time' theory, but also in Stockhausen's increasing preoccupation with information theory. Also, linked to this, the idea of the 'group' takes form. It has a longer-sustained identity, and more component parts, i.e. it can be much more complicated and yet clear. A stick is just a stick; three sticks can be a triangle. To what extent the 'time' theory remained outside musical experience, Stockhausen's and ours, or even to what extent it functioned as a prop – like Haydn's frock coat or Wagner's perfumes – providing him with the right intellectual ambience for inspiration to live in is a question no one has yet answered. Though this theory, from the vantage point of today, can be seen as Stockhausen's first inklings of the later holistic vision of universal unity, today enriched by a considerable knowledge of physics and bio-chemistry. It has now become, he claims, the 'prime mover' of his music.

Here is a summary of the theory as explained in Stockhausen's important article '. . . how time passes . . .'* Music is a series of events in time. Pitch extends from about 16 impulses a second to roughly 6,000 impulses a second. Duration extends from 8 seconds to $\frac{1}{16}$ second; 8 seconds being (according to Stockhausen) the slowest pulse used in music up to the present, 16 impulses a second being the fastest sounds we can perceive separately before they merge into pitch or quasi-pitch. Thus duration and pitch are only different areas in one time scale reaching from an impulse every eight seconds to 6,000 impulses every second. This is an obvious result of playing around with the Cologne impulse generators and experiencing the transition from slow clicks through low pitch to high pitch in a continuous glissando as the knob is turned or the tape speed increased. He uses such a transition, but the other way, as a codetta in the middle of *Kontakte*; it starts as a 'bass voice' and ends as a 'drum'. Pitch and timbre (partials) become rhythm and pitch when slowed down below 16 fundamental impulses per second.

* In *Die Reihe*, vol. 3, p. 10.

New Theories

If one is aware, as electronic composers must be, that one's pitches are proportionally related vibration speeds, then it seems quite logical that any proportions a piece uses relating durations one to another could also be applied to pitches.

The octave 1 : 2 proportion is simple. In the pitch octave there are 11 notes in between. The equivalent in duration is:

Ex. 9

This is a rhythmic monster: it is the equivalent of taking only one vibration out of each note. It is just as logical to make a series of pitch vibrations equal a series of durations. We measure by the second for pitch (c.p.s.) and by the minute for durations (metronome markings). The proportions of the two scales may be equated by dividing the metronome octave ♩ = 60 → ♩ = 120 into 12 logarithmically equal steps to equal the 12 quasi-logarithmic steps of the tempered scale. Thus, two notes whose frequencies are related by a certain numerical relationship and which each lasts a certain number of vibrations (cycles per second) could 'equal' two tempi related by the same numerical relationship, which last the same number of beats-at-that-tempo as the notes lasted cycles per second – though, of course, Stockhausen never uses the latter correspondence, which would result in an astronomically large number of beats in any one tempo.

The next step is to find the rhythmic equivalent of the overtones of fundamental pitches, obviously an important factor in the attempt to define music, or in this case 'colour', as time. If the colour or timbre of a note is defined by the strength or absence of the double, triple, quadruple (etc.) speed frequencies above it, an exact durational equivalent would be to subdivide a fundamental duration into its two halves, three thirds, four quarters (etc.) and change the 'rhythm-colour' by strengthening the volume of some subdivisions and omitting others. The only place where the quintuplets, sextuplets, etc., coincide is on their first beat, thus defining the fundamental duration as the overtones define the note.

We have, then, tempo and pitch both organised in a twelve-step chromatic scale, both of which may be organised in the twelve-note serial system. But we also have a system of rhythmic correspondence to the overtone series – a harmonic, highly tonal system. Stockhausen sees 'a fundamental contradiction between instrumental music and serial music'; he is criticising serial Schoenberg in particular (superficially actually, but that is a long story), and goes on: 'the instrumental sounds' *harmonic scale of perception* was irreconcilably opposed to the *chromatic scale of perception* of the twelve fundamental tones in the octave, whose steps were serially composed'. Therefore, he continues, we must use a *corresponding* mixture in the rhythmic sphere, to make the rhythm 'harmonic' too. Personally, I think this contradiction is more apparent than real, and that the electronic analyst cannot see listeners' wood for his own trees. The identity of a bassoon F as just that is structurally much more important than its separable (or inseparable?) component parts. However Stockhausen has ingeniously, without doubt, incorporated 'instruments playing serial music' into a neat macro-time framework of 'harmonic rhythms in serial tempi'. To maintain only one tempo would not balance the 'micro-time' or pitch events, it would be the equivalent of tonal music (having only one tonal centre, instead of many). Stockhausen fluctuates his tempi within his twelve-step scale, using 'octave transposition' by halving or doubling the metronome mark, or, of course, by halving or doubling the notation.

It is worth trying to answer the question as to whether there is any historical precedent for this apparently basic relationship between macro- and micro-rhythm. The Viennese classics are the foundation of our present day mainstream sense of musical order. If they defined the nature of satisfying structure in such an archetypal way, then it should be possible to find something of macro-micro-rhythmic relationships in their works. If the tonic poses a certain texture in duplets, one would expect the modulation to the dominant to define a speed $1\frac{1}{2}$ times as fast, since a fifth has a vibrational speed $1\frac{1}{2}$ times faster than its fundamental; in other words, triplets. Examples are not infrequent in Beethoven, but it is usually in the transition that the screwing up occurs; the second subject itself

is often restful by way of contrast to the excitement of the transition. Examples at random are: Piano Sonatas op. 14 no. 2, op. 49 no. 2, Quartets op. 59 no. 1, op. 135. It happens frequently enough in Haydn to arouse one's suspicion that he might have dimly felt the relationship, for example, in the Quartets op. 54 no. 3, op. 64 nos. 1, 5 and 6, op. 77 no. 1. Mozart uses it in two of the mature quartets, and once in the piano sonatas, where the second subject is a transposition up a fifth of the first, similarly unaccompanied, and introduces the first triplets of the piece after a long first subject and transition. The texture is then dominated by triplets.

Ex. 10

The more one studies and listens to music of this period, the more one becomes aware of the perpetual passacaglia of I–IV–(or II)–V–I progressions through every phrase, constantly transformed, now meandering, now concise, now the IV becoming elevated to a I and having its own progression – a vastly extended step in a much larger I–IV–V–I sequence – and so on. It is a fascinating hierarchy of forms within forms. In fact, macro- and micro-structures. The biggest macro-structure of all is the four movement symphony. As if moulded by natural forces (if you will pardon the teleological tone) there evolved two outer movements of roughly similar speeds in the same tonality, a slow one second, often in the subdominant, a scherzo third. Of course I am picking Beethoven from history to suit my purposes; however, we are engaged on a search for any precedents, and the Beethoven symphony is a pinnacle of symphonic form.

In the first Symphony the tonalities are I–IV–I–I (V occurs prominently, of course, but not as a fundamental tonality) and the speeds are roughly I–IV ($\frac{2}{3}$ speed)–V ($1\frac{1}{2}$ speed) in the first three movements. Beethoven's metronome marks, which, however strange his metronome, should be proportionately correct, are: 𝅗𝅥 = 112, ♪ = 120, 𝅗𝅥. = 108, 𝅗𝅥 = 88. The first three tempi are perceptibly similar. The 𝅝 of the first movement and the ♩. of the subdominant slow movement stand in a clear 3 : 2 relationship (Ex. 11).

Ex. 11

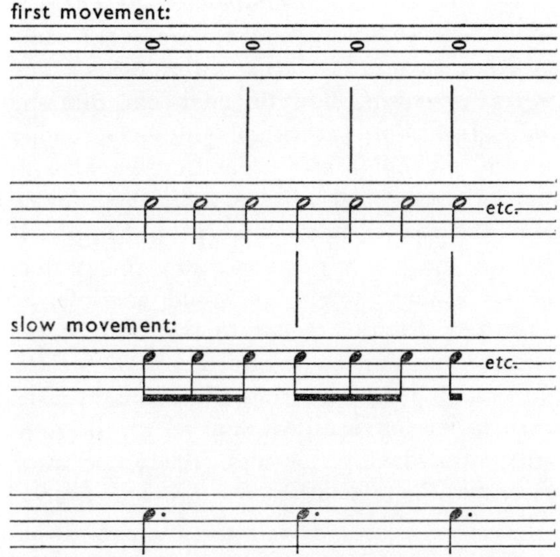

The ♩ of the scherzo stands in a clear 3 : 2 relationship with the ♩ of the first movement: 𝅗𝅥 = 112, 𝅗𝅥. = 108. The last movement doesn't fit into the picture, though it does not sound that much slower than the first (112 and 88) on account of its semiquaver bustle and its duple similarity. Here is a table of the metronome relationships in the other symphonies:

No. 2: first and scherzo relationship exactly.
3: first and slow relationship exactly.
4: first and last relationship exactly (and scherzo 20 out).
5: first and scherzo relationship nearly.
6: has five movements.
7: first and slow relationship nearly.
8: none.
9: all relationships present within 8.

These slow movements are not in the subdominant, however, except for 4, 6 and 8. But the practice was well established with Mozart, for whom it was almost a matter of course, and with Beethoven's First, so that Beethoven's later works may be seen to be a tonal jump ahead of this practice, with which he was already bored. The tension engendered by a move to the dominant exists by reason of the multiplication of all degrees by $1\frac{1}{2}$, a move to the dominant's dominant involves a further multiplication by $1\frac{1}{2}$, and so on *ad infinitum* up the sharp side. Similarly, the flat side has been shown to have subjective connotations of a 'sinking feeling' – a demotion of the tonic pivot note to the rank of mere dominant – it involves division as opposed to multiplication (for example, in the last movement of Mahler's 9th where D flat symbolises very dramatically ultimate sinking, utter rest, etc. as is suggested by its tempo and rhythm character. Or note the double progression to the *flat submediant* which becomes associated with the Adagio theme itself). The 'tension' associated with sharp sides and the 'relaxation' associated with flat sides are indications that we intuitively perceive such a correspondence as:

Ex. 12

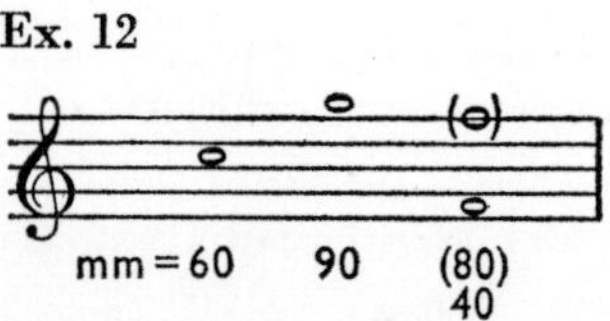

since 3 in the time of 2 or vice versa is the one change of tempo (halving or doubling tempo apart) that is familiar since the Renaissance. We may say, then, that something of the time-relationships Stockhausen's theory brought to the surface was unconsciously felt in previous music, though whether this observation is a bad case of hindsight's wisdom is still an open question, and should be tested by the listener's own feeling and experience.

The other changes of tempo are not so well-worn. We have, as Schenker has shown, to go through circles of fifths to arrive at our diatonic scale,

Ex. 13

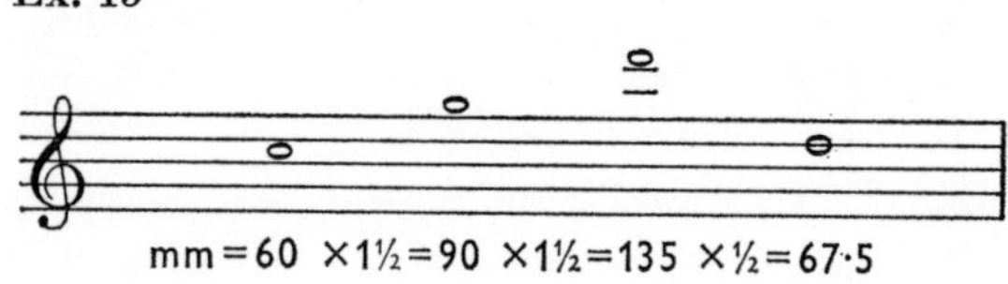

thus, in making a tempo change from 60 to 67·5, we are really going through three steps: a move to the dominant degree, a move to its dominant, and a move an octave down, or $1\frac{1}{2} \times 1\frac{1}{2} \times \frac{1}{2}$, though the third step is really irrelevant, since halving or doubling occurs with every 𝅘𝅥𝅯 𝅘𝅥𝅮 𝅘𝅥 𝅗𝅥 we meet. Schenker explains the peculiar tension of the tone step, although so ceaselessly used through the course of time for obvious reasons, by means of its distance from 'Nature'. A careful study of Schubert's *Lieder* will show that the arpeggio is associated with relaxation and, above all, freedom, and the tone or semitone step is associated with tension or constraint. Compare, for instance, *Gruppe aus dem Tartarus* with *Auf dem See* (Goethe); but usually both types appear in all songs. Stockhausen is perhaps hoping for too much in present-day ears if he supposes that they can make this tone transition in tempo. But are these hypothetical ears of the future different from our ears in kind, or in degree? They must only be different in degree, for they are capable of the fifth/$1\frac{1}{2}$ equation. Presumably, then, there is something we are missing; we are in the same position as our forefathers were when they were discovering how to 'hear' the diatonic scale. Just as we practise playing fives against sevens, we should also expand our sophistication in tempo relationships, a hitherto, for no apparent reason, neglected aspect of music. If enough music were written using the twelve-degree scale of tempi we would, in time, be educated. All this is not to say that Stockhausen has written the ideal music for the purpose; it is by no means educational music, and he has obviously despaired at the difficulty of achieving this sophistication in more recent works (exceptions are *Trans* or *Inori*).

5

Piano Pieces V–X

Piano Piece V is a beautiful, self-sufficient and rewarding addition to anybody's repertoire. It is in six sections, each one in a different, related tempo. The 'moderato' movements occur first, then the 'scherzo' movements, finally the slow movement. The classical terms are used to show that not even the most casual ear could construe this as a I–IV–V–I rhythmic structure. The tempi are 80, 90, 71, 113·5, 101, 63·5: in other words, every even step in the 'octave' scale from 60 to 120. The pitch analogy would be an arrangement of a whole tone scale, first note chosen at random,

Ex. 14

one of the two completely 'atonal' selections possible, the other being six notes of a chromatic scale. The avoidance of a tonal pattern matches the atonal pitch structure. In the other short piano pieces also, where there is not time for the whole chromatic scale of tempi, namely *Piano Pieces VII* and *VIII*, there is an incomplete 'whole tone' scale in *VII*:

Ex. 15

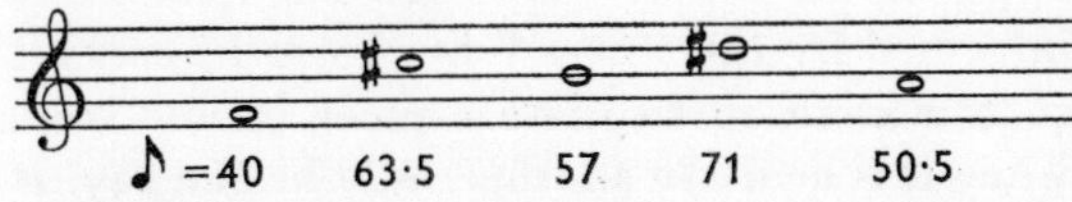

and the missing 'G' is supplied by *VIII* at the faster speed:

Ex. 16

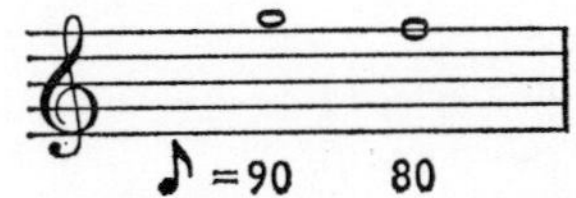

the two pieces are meant to be played together.

In *Piano Piece V* the six sections last:

60 quavers
104 quavers
38 quavers
24 quavers
84 quavers
95 quavers

To get an idea of the relative weight of the sections when tempi and metrical length of section combine, we may draw up a rough table in seconds:

45 seconds
70 seconds
32 seconds
13 seconds
50 seconds
90 seconds

Thus, the last, slow section becomes easily the longest, although it has fewer quaver beats than the second. This is for a reason. For the same reason, it is also the least dense, having only one attack per second on average: section two has nearly twice as many ($1\frac{6}{7}$). The densities consistently follow the proportion of the section as measured in seconds, not as measured in quavers, as might be expected. The shorter the section in seconds, the more notes per second; this is in spite of the tempo – see, for instance, section three, which has the second slowest tempo, but the second highest density, because it is the second shortest. The average densities for the six sections run:

$2\frac{1}{9}$ attacks per second
$1\frac{6}{7}$ attacks per second
3 attacks per second
$3\frac{1}{3}$ attacks per second
$1\frac{3}{4}$ attacks per second
1 attack per second

Thus, in a piece that sounds predominantly like recitative, dense spots occur in the short sections in the middle of the piece, or, to be more precise, at the ends of the third and fourth sections, and spilling over into the beginning of the fifth, a longer section, but in the second fastest tempo. The rest of this penultimate section, however, is dominated by silences which increase to the end of the piece. Here is a satisfying shape, somewhat akin to scales of excitement in *early* sonata form, where, very roughly, exposition is medium, development is high (counterpoint density, modulation density), recapitulation is lower (repetition of the known, modulatory repose except for altered transition), and coda is lowest (self-repetitious, tonally static). The last section is thus slow, long and sparse in order to function like a coda.

Each section is compounded of several groups. There is variety in the length and distinctiveness of these groups. They stretch from one single, short note in the sixth section near the end, to forty-seven notes in the third section. They are sometimes articulated by silence, sometimes seem to merge with another group, and one loses one's sense of articulation momentarily. In this interplay lies the great fantasy of the piece. The number of groups per section is roughly proportionate to the lengths of the sections. The first, third and fourth sections contain steadily fewer groups, while the second and the last two remain constant at about 14 or 15 (Ex. 17).

We may in theory, at least, draw satisfaction from perceiving a progression placed against an unchanging repetition. This whole principle, that some elements change much more quickly than others is an important one for Stockhausen: *Plus Minus* is a blueprint for such a principle.

All I have said about the six sections in *Piano Piece V* is subject to a certain degree of disguise, because not only are there many ritardandi and accelerandi, but the changes of tempo are not always apparent at the beginnings of the new sections, either because of syncopation or of grace notes which interrupt the metrical flow. So, of course, the feeling of six clear-cut sections of a certain length is more apparent on paper than to the ear, unless it is informed by the score. Why it was important to Stockhausen to write a piece in one way, when it is heard in another, only he can say. It

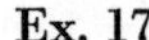
Ex. 17

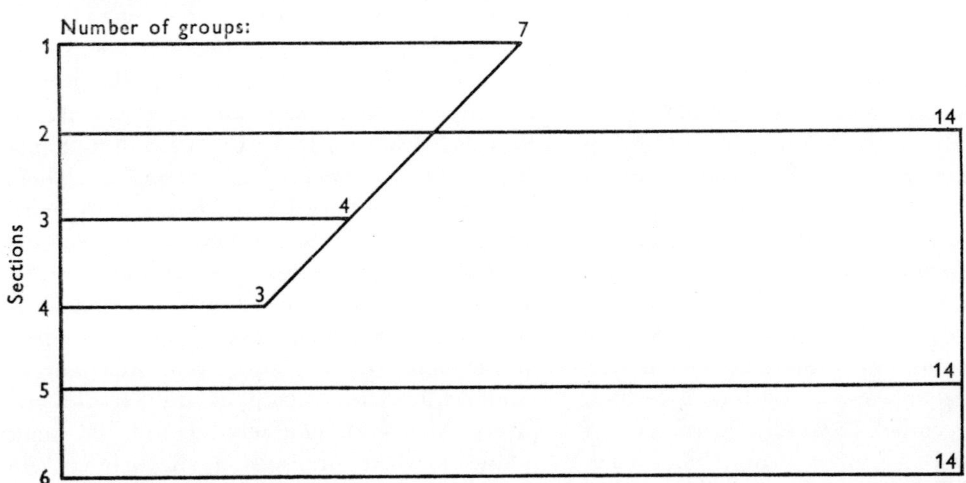

points to the suspicion that theory and musicality are not yet one. At any rate, the discrepancy becomes less and less frequent in subsequent scores because he evades the whole issue and turns to other things.

What is most apparent to the ear, however, is the occurrence of three types of 'character groups'. The first type is largely written in demisemiquavers, and uses repetition of pitches (from nine to eighteen of them). The second type consists of isolated, rich, almost romantic, chords in the middle register. The third type consists of successions of low, gruff, short chords with varied, pointillistic dynamics. All three are exposed in the first section. The third section is outstandingly full of character, in that it contains all three types in a short space of time, and the second type is played twice. The last section outstandingly lacks character, in that it only has one character group once (romantic chord). The other sections have two or three character groups selected from two of the three possible types only. Again, therefore, one perceives a central climax of interest and a coda which winds down.

The first type of group appears in the first four sections. In the first section it is a uniform *ff*, in the second a uniform *pp*, in the third ten dynamics are used, each note being separately marked, and the same note is never repeated with the same dynamic. The interest is therefore shifted to the parameter of dynamics. The sudden static quality of multiple pedals, pitch invention at its lowest, is a most distinctive feature of Stockhausen's style. Again, this idea hit Stockhausen's consciousness through information theory and a study of Webern. He wrote: 'A process usually very important for the time-moulding in Webern's music is the fixing of each note in a constant octave-register, and alternation of registers at the most varying speeds; this is one of the most notable means of moulding experiential time. . . .'* Compare, for instance, the repetition of bottom C sharp (and A sharp) in *Piano Piece VII*, where the same note is played eight times in succession, each time not only with a different dynamic and mode of attack, but also with different and often remote harmonics produced by silently depressing different notes. Other examples occur in *Kontra-Punkte*, in the middle of *Refrain*, throughout *Gruppen*, in *Piano Piece VI* (p. 24), and even, chordally, in *Piano Piece X*, and in much of the later music where they become fixed pitches for improvisation. The fourth time the group appears, in the fourth section, it again has varied dynamics consisting of short crescendi and decrescendi. Thus each appearance is dynamically different.

There is a similar pattern in the pitch parameter. The first statement of the group consists of ten pitches, but because there are two Cs only nine pitch classes (G, G sharp and A being omitted). The second statement consists of fifteen pitches, and eleven pitch classes, G sharp being omitted. The third statement is the clearest. Here we have all twelve pitch classes, and twelve pitches (no octave doublings). This is classical perfection, from which the others may be said to deviate, though, to compensate, dynamically it is the most spiky and irregular. The fourth statement has eighteen pitches, and all the twelve pitch classes. Two statements lead up to this 'classical' statement, 9 → 11 → 12 pitch classes, and the last one diffuses it. Similarly,

* 'Structure and Experiential Time', *Die Reihe*, vol. 2, p. 72.

the first statement has only three 'foreign' notes that are not repeated, the second seven, the third none, and the fourth has as many unrepeated notes as repeated ones. In this central third statement all notes are played four or five times. In all the other statements the notes are repeated in unequal numbers with increasing diffuseness. The last statement, being short, using the maximum twelve pitch classes, using more pitches, having a much wider span, repeating only a few notes, is almost in danger of not being recognised as belonging to its genre, and thus merges finally into the texture of the rest of the piece. The first character group, in sum, makes a clear progression throughout the piece.

The second character group, the rich, middle register chord, has a rather more complex history. This is not surprising since it is so easily recognised: it stands out from the one-note-at-a-time texture like a tree on a plain, and it is a more 'familiar' gesture than any of the others, what psychologists call a *Gestalt*. Here the first appearance is the clearest, an isolated chord of five notes, their individual dynamics being gently differentiated between *p* and *pppp*, possible if carefully fingered. It has a slight stringency, with three semitone clashes, displaced by one or two octaves. It changes subsequently in the following ways: in section two it occurs with an anacrusis twice, this being once at the bottom of the chord, once above it. Immediately after the first group there is a four chord development preceded by a large anacrusis (five notes), very loud. This group repeats many of the pitches used just before, either in the previous chord, or before that in the previous texture, and so has the effect of *repeating* in a chordal style, rather than of achieving an important climax, which would be inappropriate so soon in the piece. Nevertheless, for this type of texture, the chordal, it is a moment of glory. In the third section the group occurs with an even more powerful anacrusis. The nine notes heard together (the pedal sustains the anacrusis) comprise the most dissonant chord of the piece (six semitone clashes), but the impact is lessened by the fact that the notes are spread out into four attacks. The variety of presentation of this group is fascinating. Also in section three, there is a *piano* chord of only four notes which almost doesn't count because it is not very isolated, and has only two semitone clashes. It has the function of repeating four notes just heard rather indistinctly four octaves lower; in particular an adjacent semitone clash, the only one in the piece, which reappears at the top of it. Again the same group is playing radically different roles.

In the fourth section we have a chord similar in pitch and dynamics to the first chord of the piece. The only real difference is that the attacks are spread into three instead of being simultaneous. Its role is recapitulation.

In the fifth section there is an even bigger variation than before. The chord rises directly from a character group of the third type. The low, gruff chords rise in pitch to unite gradually with the identity of the isolated middle register chord, which is nevertheless quite unmistakable. Thus a traditional type pun is made. Further on in this section occurs an eight-note chord, containing *six* semitone clashes. Since it contains only three vertical attacks, all *ff*, it is consequently the most violent chord in the piece.

The coda's chord contains only three semitone clashes, is marked *mp*, and therefore helps the other winding down processes at this point. The history of this character group within the piece is therefore one of a constantly inventive variety of functions, ranging from recapitulation to one or two well spaced climaxes.

Of the third type of character group, consisting of low, gruff chords, it is only necessary to say that it occurs three times – in the first section, in the characterful third section, and in the fifth; and that the second statement is twice the first (twice as many chords, each dynamic twice instead of once), and the third statement develops further by being short and by diffusing the character with grace notes until, again, it is scarcely recognisable. So this group-type and the first, repeated-pitch one display clear developmental patterns, while the second group-type is static in behaviour, in the sense that a kaleidoscope is static. Once again, movement and stillness are used to articulate each other.

I have touched on section form and group form; it now remains to consider the pitch. The shape of the organism depends on the speed at which new pitches are introduced. The character group of repeated pitches is the beginning of a scale which extends from *that* to the situation in which every note is a different pitch for a stretch of twenty or thirty notes, and in which all twelve pitch classes are fairly evenly employed as well.

The general texture is dominated by internal pedals, pitches which occur more often than any others. 'The unknown must come out of the known.' Each new group contains a few actual pitches from the previous group or groups, and adds varying quantities of its own. Thus different types of group are connected together in unexpected ways, there is a continuous counterpoint between pitch and group character, not dissimilar to what in Schoenberg is a counterpoint between twelve-note set and thematic material, and in tonal music between tonality and thematic material. The repetitions occur in carefully calculated proportions. From the first section to the second to the third there is a crescendo of repetition. The third contains the long repeated note group at its end, preceded by the gruff chords group, one of whose characteristics it is to keep a number of pitches constant; thus repetition is elevated here to its clearest audibility. Each note is played, on average, $2\frac{1}{7}$ times in section one, $2\frac{2}{7}$ times in section two, and three times in section three. Of the eighty-eight pitches possible on the piano, Stockhausen uses only thirty-three for all of the ninety-five attacks in section three, a fairly stringent limitation. In this sort of style, Stockhausen's careful selection of the pitches he needs is the characteristic which distinguishes him most from his contemporaries, with the notable exception of Boulez. Witness his early experiences in the significantly unlimited field of electronic music as shown in *Studie 1*, which is even fuller of internal pedals than the piano pieces.

For the next two sections we drop to a much lower average rate of repetition, $1\frac{4}{7}$ and $1\frac{1}{3}$. These two penultimate sections tell us most, and are the most difficult to take in, which is fitting at this point. From the least repetitious we return finally to the medium level of repetitiousness, from $1\frac{1}{3}$ to $2\frac{1}{4}$, which is also fitting, as the coda is a relaxation in every way, of tempo, of density, of character, and of the new-note-to-old ratio.

To sum up, the shape of the piece is as follows. The first section is exposition, the second is a start to progression in various directions. The last section is obviously a coda for the reasons stated above. Sections three, four and five each form a climax for one or more of the dimensions. In section three the *character groups* all appear in quick succession, linked by common pitches, and *repetitiousness* at the same time reaches its climax. In section four we have the *fastest*, *densest* and *shortest* section, and in section five we have the climax of *pitch information*, i.e. least repetition. Thus the interest is sustained in different ways throughout.

The idea of riveting the listener's attention on one dimension is an important one for understanding Stockhausen's mind, and it becomes vastly expanded in the more recent works where the 'groups' become 'moments'.

I should finally mention, with regard to *Piano Piece V*, the serialisation of freedom. The grace notes, which exist independently of the tempo, have their own scale of speeds, depending on how awkward they are to play clearly. They are played 'freely', but it is a freedom dependent on musical exigencies, such as the instrument and the acoustics of the room. The eighth piano piece exemplifies the two types of tempo perfectly, as it consists of only one element (contrapuntal lines) and grace notes (chords). The two pursue a frantic and exciting dialogue, now independent, now meeting.*

The question of how much serialism there is, is difficult, because in many contexts there is no *perceptible* serial system (which we can assert with authority), but we would risk contradiction from the composer if we said there was no serial system. In other words, there is no passage of music ever written that cannot be accounted for by some sort of seriality, therefore unless one knows the composer's mind there is strictly speaking always a risk of falsehood. It is obviously impossible to follow a series of modes of pedalling, or modes of attack, or a series of technical difficulty, but I think that we should not try to 'follow' a series in the way we do in Schoenberg and Webern. What matters is that we are aware of a scale between two extremes being used in an artistically varied way, avoiding too much repetition except on the large scale that defines that it is a scale of so many steps. A clear, systematic example of this is *Piano Piece XI*, where scales of six tempi, six modes of attack and six dynamics are applied at random to nineteen groups: we perceive the extents of the scales, but their order, interestingly varied, is not strictly serial. One of Stockhausen's virtues is that he uses more scales of organisation in full consciousness than any previous composer.

It is, however, clear that Stockhausen means by serialism something rather different from what Schoenberg, Webern and Babbitt, for instance, mean by it. Stockhausen is as interested in using a mode, or repertoire, of graded possibilities ('the mediation between two extremes') as he is in making clear a repeated ordering of that repertoire. That it should be repeated is a necessary condition of the intelligibility of *ordering* as something of compositional significance, as opposed to mere occurrence. In tonal music each pitch had at least two basic meanings: it stood in an intervallic relationship with its fellow pitches and it stood in a tonal relationship with some tonic. (E.g. 'a third above x *and* the subdominant degree of tonality y'.) Schoenberg's free atonalism tried desperately and magnificently to get round the lack of the second of these qualities with drama and violence of expression; and then, in the serial works, he substituted ordering. (E.g. 'a third above x *and* the fourth note of the series'.) Unless the double meaning of each note is made clear by the composer the significance of the music is less by half, or at least the pitch part of it is. Stockhausen certainly pays homage to 'ordering', but only now and again, and the temptation to debase the currency of pitch in exciting new colouristic textures and (electronically) in 'noise' is too seductive to be resisted; though it must be said that the exhaustion of a graded repertoire of possibilities in dimensions other than pitch through the course of a piece is one of Stockhausen's most impressive musical achievements.

The other piano pieces also exploit six new modes of attack, which Stockhausen compares with the 'series of envelope curves' used in *Studie 1*. Each of these pieces exploits a very distinct and individual form, however, which does not impinge on any other.

---

* For further discussion of the serialisation of freedom, see below, p. 47ff.

Piano Piece VI, for example, has a distinct transition from the world of *Piano Pieces I–IV* and *Kontra-Punkte* to the world of group character, of *Gruppen* and the later piano pieces. The long first part is very difficult for similar reasons to those mentioned in connection with *Piano Pieces I–IV*, but gradually character identity is sustained a little longer; now it is chords, now fixed pitch pedals, now silences and single notes and certain intervals, now a single pedal (middle D sharp), now chromatic grace notes up or down to a terminal goal, now the tempo – expressed by a wavy line moving on a 13-line stave representing 13 tempi from 45 → 180 (a typical manifestation of Stockhausen's love for exact visual equivalents) – becomes more purposeful with lines such as:

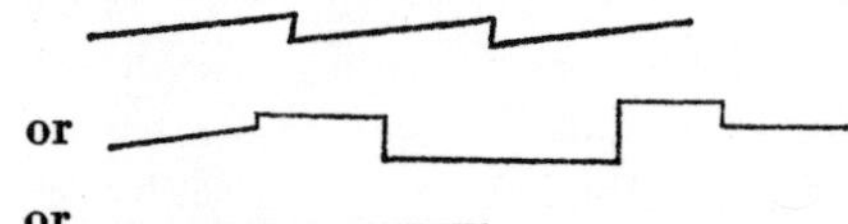

and so on. Interestingly, some of these character identities, such as grace notes, are the result of a revision, for Stockhausen came increasingly to care about this sort of differentiation.

*Piano Piece VII** again uses different material: all types of harmonics – some very far up the series – are obtained by depressing keys silently. The piece needs to be heard at very close quarters to be fully effective. Middle C sharp dominates the first section as a fixed pitch, and is treated in the second tempo section (see above p. 35) by omission, in the third by being placed in four registers, in the fourth by being fixed three octaves lower (with A sharp), and also by omission, and in the fifth by being fixed one octave higher (with D sharp). One can tell an 'omission' by the fact that Stockhausen goes through the 85 pitch classes of the first section – the 'text' – to generate the rest of the piece – 'variation' – adding occasional repetitions and grace note additions. He uses the same symmetrical set as the one he uses later in *Gruppen*. For a discussion of it see below (p. 56). Here he only uses the set and five symmetrically chosen transpositions, which link in a Webern-like manner in that the last note of one set is the same as the beginning of the next set. However, as in *Gruppen*, the sets do not, except for the first and final ones, start with the first note, but with one in the middle.

At the expense, I am afraid, of the splendid eighth and ninth pieces, I would like to try to give a bird's eye view of *Piano Piece X*, which is considerably longer and grander in conception than anything discussed so far. Although it belongs primarily to the set called Nr. 4 (*Piano Pieces V–X*, 1954–5), both it and *Piano Piece IX* were not written out until 1961.

Obvious peculiarities of the notation are: no section lines, instead durations written in the space above the staves within which the given music must be fitted, and a thick line (as for quavers, conventionally) to which all notes are connected by stems and which slopes upward for accelerando and downward for ritardando, all notes' durations being indicated by the length of a slur. This notation implies that there is great rhythmic freedom within rather

* I should like to acknowledge some helpful suggestions made to me about this piece by Christopher Wintle.

precise boundaries. An imprecise scale of things enclosed by a precise one. Any rhythmic or durational argument must therefore come through only in these boundary-defining durations above the stave, of which the rest is a varied filling. Apart from the large scale form which emerges in the way I will show below, and the fact that the longest durations always manifest themselves as the extraordinary Cage-like silences or near-silences which articulate this form, these durations have no obvious sequential pattern. At the most (and rather academically), we can say that they lie, if plotted on log/ordinary graph paper, on sinusoidal curves – not one but several – with an exactness that seems more likely to be rational than random; but this must necessarily be pretty remote, except in a general sense of sequential alternation, from the auditory experience.

The material used is the following:

1. single-voice chromatic or semi-chromatic darting fragments, terminating often in some goal note
2. 2-part chords *pp* } dynamics some-
3. 3-part chords *p* } times swopped
4. 4-part chords *mf*
5. 5-part chords *f* } dynamics some-
6. 6-part chords *ff* } times swopped
7. 7-part chords *fff*

Seven widths of cluster, including:

8. clusters played with the fingers
9. clusters played with the hand(s)
10. clusters played with the forearm(s)
11. finger cluster glissando (gloves are recommended)
12. hand cluster glissando
13. arpeggio up
14. arpeggio down
15. rapidly repeated notes and clusters
16. one trill!
17. half pedal to reverberate sounds softly
18. silent depression of the forearm cluster in bass to reverberate sounds softly
19. silent depression of keys immediately after attack to reverberate sounds softly.

The main idea of the piece is a big gesture followed by tiny isolated vestiges or after-echoes of it. The quasi-sonata-form of the whole structure is as follows:

1. Big opening group followed by six isolated vestiges of 'single-voice chromatic' and six of clusters (fairly large vestiges).
2. Three increasingly long sections, each prefaced by increasingly short single chromatic, and made up of cluster and chord groups. Followed by several isolated vestiges of them. Each of these sections may be summed up as (∪–∪∪∪∪) in terms of scansion.
3. Big 'recapitulatory' group (blowing up an insignificant figure, repeated notes, to enormous proportions, but this is an exceptional technique), followed by isolated vestiges.

Then follow three more big groups with their vestiges, but these are less isolated and refer also to ideas other than those occurring in the big group immediately before. The big groups become increasingly shorter themselves, and effect a general mixture and gentle disintegration or liquidation, as Schoenberg would say, of the hitherto very separate elements. If this is like a coda, we might call the first section exposition, the second development and the third recapitulation. After group 1, the groups are articulated in serial manner by the varying emphases laid on seven character-types built out of the elementary material listed above.

A more detailed look at some of the ways this general plan is carried out may be helpful. The single-voice chromatic *ppp* element retains its identity almost throughout the piece by staying below that part of the piano which does not damp and above the area where such speed would sound murky. It starts at the very beginning of the piece with an expression of the first six notes of the same set as Stockhausen uses in *Piano Piece VII* and *Gruppen* (amongst other places), at first in the subsidiary decorative notes which quickly depart from it, then, transposed, in the structural notes, notated with larger note heads, which are sustained like a cantus firmus. The rest of this first group is a most extraordinary outburst of 'maximum information', everything on the list is included, and there are no articulative silences; the only concession Stockhausen makes to the 'redundancy' the ear craves (and this alone puts the passage quite apart from the 'difficulty' of the first piano piece or the beginning of the sixth) is that for short periods of time the same element is continuously used – strings of, say, ten chords of the same size and dynamic.

Tacked right on to the end of this is the first of the six vestiges of the single chromatic element. It is very close to the opening statement of this element, not only in that it repeats the two serial hexachords, the decorative and the cantus firmus, at the identical transpositions, and paraphrases other figurations too, but also in that it has virtually the same length. But in the second case half of this length is occupied by the quiet reverberation of four notes with no new attacks. One might call it a first subject codetta (at the risk of Procrustean bedism) which rounds off the first part of the exposition with a reference back. It is certainly a sort of Janus's door, and in that capacity a unique and effective structure. After the unrelieved violence of the opening pages this and the sudden prolonged silence which follows are dramatic in the extreme. Here is Stockhausen's structural thinking at its best.

After these six single chromatic vestiges come the six cluster vestiges, likewise all separated by silence or reverberation. They, too, suggest ternary thinking in that the middle ones are made up of hand and finger clusters (with glissandi), but the first and last use the violent *forearm* clusters (with glissandi), developed in the last one to an aggressive peak. This gives birth to a very long pause indeed while the sounds fade away only to be interrupted by element 7, one *fff* 7-part chord with a single high note after it leaving in its wake another sea of dying reverberation. This lonely lighthouse of a sound is likewise magnificently dramatic, for we have not heard anything resembling a sonorously spaced chord since the very opening group. Again, Stockhausen's love of 'Germanic' chords, as Boulez is supposed pejoratively to have called them! Again, the typical brief gesture in an opposite direction at the end of a section – a feature of this rather strict piece on all its levels. Again, also, the two-faced element which looks back into its 'own' section and forward to the development in which chords are again going to appear.

Now for the 'development'. Three sections follow, each introduced by an ever shorter passage of single chromatic (as at the opening of the work), each section one page longer – the notation is proportionate to the time it lasts, so this is a rough guide. The liquidation of the single chromatic element is given further relevance by the fact that the group that is liquidated is virtually the same length as those single chromatic statements which opened and closed the big first block, and has initially the same amount of played music (as opposed to reverberations) – 9½ crochets – too.

Here is a chart of the 'development':

The reader can see the various symmetries and near-symmetries resulting from a division of the third section of the development. It is both one section and two, there are interesting pressures on us to hear it as both, as already demonstrated. Sections 1 and 3a, have much in common, and in addition to similarities obvious from the chart below, they are the only two sections to have *arpeggiated* chords.

Now for the last part of the work. The characteristics of the four component sections are as

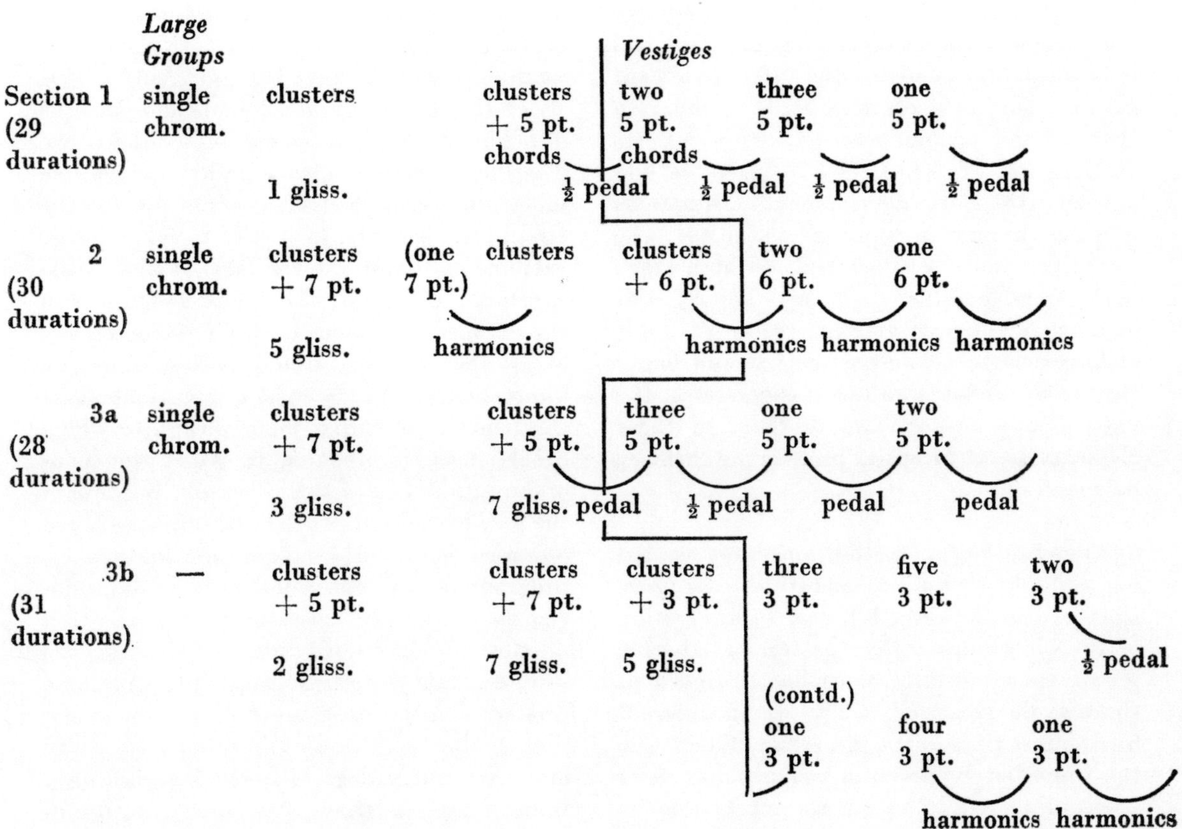

follows. Sections one and two liquidate once and for all that idea of the single chromatic texture as a *preface*, so that it does not appear *before* section three at all, but is changed in the middle of that section, by means of cross-breeding with another element (the hand cluster), from its delicate and dry nervousness into a sound like Indian bells, high and pedalled and softer than any other notes in the piece. It emerges from the pitches of the hand cluster like a butterfly from the chrysalis.

Section one is recapitulatory in that it is large and recapitulates the repeated note figure, and it is constantly changing the type of element in use, showing a complex aspect similar to that of the opening section. However, its vestiges (six of them) tend to resemble and develop the short 'development' vestiges as much as the large ones of the 'exposition'. The 'recapitulation's' vestiges tend to be a stage more unpredictable than any before. For instance, if the preceding big group was built of finger clusters, two-part chords and finger cluster glissandos in different successions, the vestige may contain two or three of these elements *simultaneously*, prolonging them as harmonics too.

Section two continues the same process, but has only five vestiges, and those not very isolated. Section three is a near-disintegration of the big group/vestiges pattern, as the big group, though still recognisable, is almost as short as the 'vestiges', which are all different for the first time in the piece; they don't echo the immediately preceding sounds but refer back all over the piece in the most complex way. Section four continues the disintegration

of pattern so that there is no real big group at all, merely hand clusters with four- and five-part chords growing out of them (a merging of the differences between the elements), and four final soft vestige-like four-part chords. These are strongly direction-orientated, unlike the usual backward-looking vestiges – in the upwards motion of a wedge structure of which interspersed single bass notes provide the downwards motion.

The tenth piano piece has a clear but elaborate structure. The beauty of these last four sections would not have been so great had the strict differentiations of elements and patterns of behaviour not been so carefully adhered to. There is an artistic discipline here which one must admire, a successful 'serial' use of the structural elements. Less easy to take are the extremes of crudity – the lack of small-scale rhythmic argument, the high-handedness in the detailed treatment of pitch, which on top of all the clusters often leaves a simplistic impression, certainly when one remembers the felicities of earlier piano pieces, to which Stockhausen is prepared to go at the 'non-organisation' end of the spectrum. Because of the way he talks about the oscillation between 'organisation' and 'non-organisation' in his programme note one wonders if he has sufficiently sensed the monistic nature, the grey absence of harmonic multi-meanings, the 'tidiness' and over-easy graspability of these clusters. Clusters are not complex phenomena; they bulldoze all musical relationships away and have many degrees fewer of significance than a simple triad. As Boulez wrote of clusters: 'This quickly "parcelled" material is no guarantee of great acuteness of conception; it suggests, on the contrary, a strange weakness for being satisfied with undifferentiated acoustic organisms.'* But, on the large scale, the clarity, the grandeur, and above all, the originality – the feeling that, once again, Stockhausen has fully defined a substantial idea that one says in retrospect someone had to do, it had never been done before, and now it has been so thoroughly done that nobody else can do it without appearing second hand – all this is some achievement.

* *Boulez on Music Today*, Faber, 1971, p. 44.

6
Zeitmasze

In discussing *Piano Piece V*, I mentioned briefly the 'serialisation of freedom'. Nr. 5, *Zeitmasze* (1956) for flute, oboe, clarinet, cor anglais and bassoon takes ideas on this subject much further. These ideas were also prompted by an urge to develop beyond total serialisation's discrete arithmetical (or exponential) steps in a chosen scale.* In strict total serialisation, 'Every individual magnitude had to be exactly measured, and fixed by a discrete value in each dimension (one pitch, one duration, one loudness).'† The complexity of the resulting notation often baffled the performers into playing some passages much more inaccurately than others. One should not be discouraged by this, says Stockhausen, rather one should make a virtue of it, control it and serialise it. This is surely the essence of live performed music as opposed to electronic music; composers should not urge the performer to become a machine, rather to become more human. The degrees of inaccuracy are not of the arithmetical discrete step type, but form a continuum, especially when more than one player is involved and one of the company gets gradually further and further out – an experience every chamber music player knows to his cost. He calls these areas of inaccuracy 'fields' and the size of the 'scatter' 'field-sizes'. Stockhausen must have arrived at these views by just such experiences; 'like all the reflections described those that follow have been triggered off by "purely coincidental" processes in earlier compositions. One wrote something or other, and was then startled by the way certain things hung together. Differentiated field-sizes had, in fact, already been presented, even with the normal signs for notation.

'There was the small note, for one, written independently of the other, measured time-values – the "grace-note". If its tempo was "as fast as possible", and if it were not only single but came in groups of various sizes, either before, over or after a measured time-duration, then these groups of grace-notes would take over the function of a second time-stratum "fading in" to the measured durations. Here, each individual grace-note in the group received its own field-value in time, determined in the following way: the pitches of a group were distributed on the piano in such a way that the player's hand had to make movements of very different magnitudes over

* In the first sketch version the piece simply consisted of all the metrically notated sections. The rhythmic freedoms were a later development.

† *Die Reihe*, vol. 3, p. 29.

the keyboard. The larger the pitch-interval, the larger the time-interval from note to note, for everything was to be played "as fast as possible". Besides this, the instructions mention the fact that each note should be distinctly recognisable in pitch, thus automatically making the lower notes somewhat longer than the higher ones. Thus, instead of notating all the various notations one used performing indications of a quite different kind, in order to produce a proportional *series* of field-sizes within the groups of grace-notes. The size-relationships of such a series depend, of course, on the time it takes for respective performers to react, and also on the instrument, and on space (the more resonant the room, the more slowly the grace-notes must be played, if they are not to become indistinct); but just because of this, the composed proportions continue to exist.'* If this describes what happens in the piano pieces, here is a description of its development into *Zeitmasze* and *Gruppen*: 'The longer two orchestras play in different tempi, the more probable it is that the time-strata will get out of step, be displaced. Even apart from the fact that such displacements require a corresponding control of field-harmony, field-intensity, field-density, etc., the method of time-composition must aim at regulating such *field-times*. Clearly, the flow of time can no longer be imagined as "quantified"; displacement can come about gradually and continuously within particular time-fields, and the associated field-sizes cannot be thought of as a sort of *discrete* succession.'† And, with reference to the division of a fundamental note value into its 'harmonic' subdivisions or formants (two halves, three thirds, four quarters, etc.), he writes: 'If the single time quanta of the formants are no longer in a constant relation to each other, but speed up or slow down, moreover in various degrees, then the formant-rhythm becomes more or less diffuse. Different field-sizes result according to the number of *variable tempi in the formants*, and according to the degree of their alterations, in which the original harmonic phase-relationships can no longer be traced back to a scale of *discrete* time-quanta. For example: a first duration-formant has a constant tempo, a second "as fast as possible", a third speeds up and a fourth slows down and all are to be played simultaneously; and only the fundamental duration of such a time-spectrum is exactly measured as a single value.' The five instruments play together in time at one end of the scale and all out of time at the other – this latter extreme creating a 'mass structure' where the only sense of time is the length of the whole passage – the equivalent of 'noise' in the pitch sphere, where there is no periodicity in the vibrations. In between these extremes the 'field-size' is determined by the number of instruments out of time and the degree to which they are out of time. The same scale has always existed in musicians' minds, he writes; composers compose freely or schematically, compositions are free or strict forms, performers give free or strict interpretations; and all these scales should now be used consciously in their full richness. Or rather, to push the theory to its *ne plus ultra*, not only 'consciously', but in a scale ranging from 'consciously' to 'intuitively' with all the steps in between. Similarities with the Lévi-Strauss type of grid are not hard to see.

* *Die Reihe*, vol. 3, p. 34.
† *Die Reihe*, vol. 3, p. 31.

The distinction between precise arithmetical and imprecise continuous scales (Babbitt calls them ordinal and nominal scales) is an important one, and the inclusion of the second type in later works one of the most illuminating aspects of Stockhausen's mature serialism – it is much more realistic than the imposed precision where no precision is necessary of some of the pointillistic works, Stockhausen's and others'.

Interestingly, in this 1956 article from which I have been quoting, he moots the possibility of applying field-sizes to pitch, e.g. – field duration from $\frac{1}{440}''$ to $\frac{1}{550}''$ – i.e. a possible pitch between A above middle C and the C sharp which lies a major third above it, a technique he used before the article in the composition of *Gesang der Jünglinge*. There would, of course, have been nothing new about it in a non-theorised context since the time of Schoenberg's *Sprechgesang*, for instance, to say nothing of early aleatoric scores.

So much for the theories of time as expressed in the article. In the music Stockhausen uses the following five time-measurements (*Zeitmaße* = time-measurements or tempi) which can be distributed round the five instruments.
1. Metronome-measured time, with the familiar chromatic scale of twelve tempi per octave, i.e. from a speed to its double speed. He changes tempo in a quasi-serial succession only at the beginning and end, but never in strict sequence in the *Gruppen* sense (see below). Each of the twelve tempi does appear, but six of them only once. In the middle tempi are occasionally presented simultaneously.
2. The instruction 'as fast as possible'. This applies to the speed at which one can perform the shortest notes of the passage. Obviously, there may be long durations as well, which may seem as if in a slow tempo.
3. The instruction 'as slow as possible, in one breath'. This means a passage or group-field whose time has to be estimated as a whole, and the parts then fitted inside that whole in the right proportions of note value. The other instruments take this instrument's choice of tempo as their normative tempo on these occasions.
4. The instruction 'fast – slow down' means an even progression from maximum speed to about four times as slow over the group-field-size, which may be short or long, and therefore either violent or gradual.
5. The instruction 'slow – get faster', the reverse of No. 4 (above).

This carefully thought-out plan of time and tempo pays dividends in *Zeitmasze*, where there are only up to five clear lines in any texture, more so than in any other work of Stockhausen's. Never has the intention been so clearly audible. One of the rarest things to be achieved in our avant-garde situation is genuine life and lightning-fast invention in more than one part or layer at a time, as opposed to the more usual succession of blocks or textures. Where he wants it – and he sometimes wants the opposite, homogeneity – Stockhausen's lines have a character which makes for real counterpoint of the most exciting sort. They have enough redundancy (= internal repetition of shapes, dynamic patterns, rhythmic patterns, metrical regularity etc. = strong recognisability) to avoid being muddled with competing lines, and enough new information (= irregularity =

surprises generally) to be artistically interesting. Once players have mastered their arithmetic and give instinctive performances of such lines as this:

Ex. 18

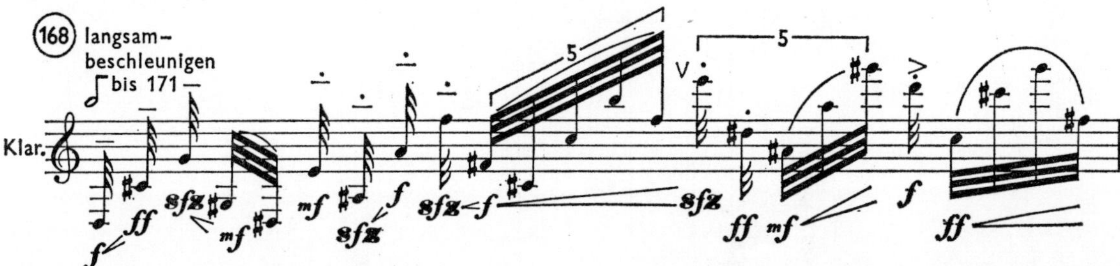

their performance, because not shackled to strict synchronisation with others, will be virtuosic, brilliant, daring and physically exhilarating in effect.

The various passages relate to each other in many dimensions, not just in the seriality of their strict proportions. Very impressive is the logic with which elements grow or disintegrate over several sections, such elements as silence, flutter-tongue, melismata, pointillism (single notes isolated and dynamically differentiated), 'melody'-like lines, etc. As Genevieve Marcus has shown at some length,* contour-motives are used with some consistency. In fact, I might add, in a manner not unlike certain works with free motivic interaction of Schoenberg and Webern. Here is an early place where these sort of motives begin to appear (Ex. 19).

Compare this with the Webern excerpt (Example 7), and trace the several wide-interval downwards arpeggios of three and four notes and finally, with the pitch and text climax, of five notes. The Stockhausen has exactly the same sort of approach to non-systematised shapeliness. Equally impressive are the movements towards and away from chordal passages. Of course, this is just a function of the field-size seriality, one of the manifestations of 'field-size = 0'. These are some of the few places where one feels the influence of Messiaen, with whom he studied twice a week for a year in 1952 and whose extraordinarily powerful musical personality so often transforms all who come near it (Exx. 20 and 21).

The last fifty-nine bars of *Zeitmasze* read like a direct introduction to the world of *Gruppen*, for as in that work the bar lines define the length of a fundamental rhythmic unit, the from-this-point-on quasi-serial tempi define the 'frequency' of those fundamentals, and the harmonic subdivisions of the fundamental bar, consistent throughout each tempo-section, define the 'group spectrum'. And that technique leads us on to Nr. 6, *Gruppen*.

* Genevieve Marcus, 'Stockhausen's *Zeitmasze*', *The Music Review*, May 1968, p. 146ff.

Ex. 19

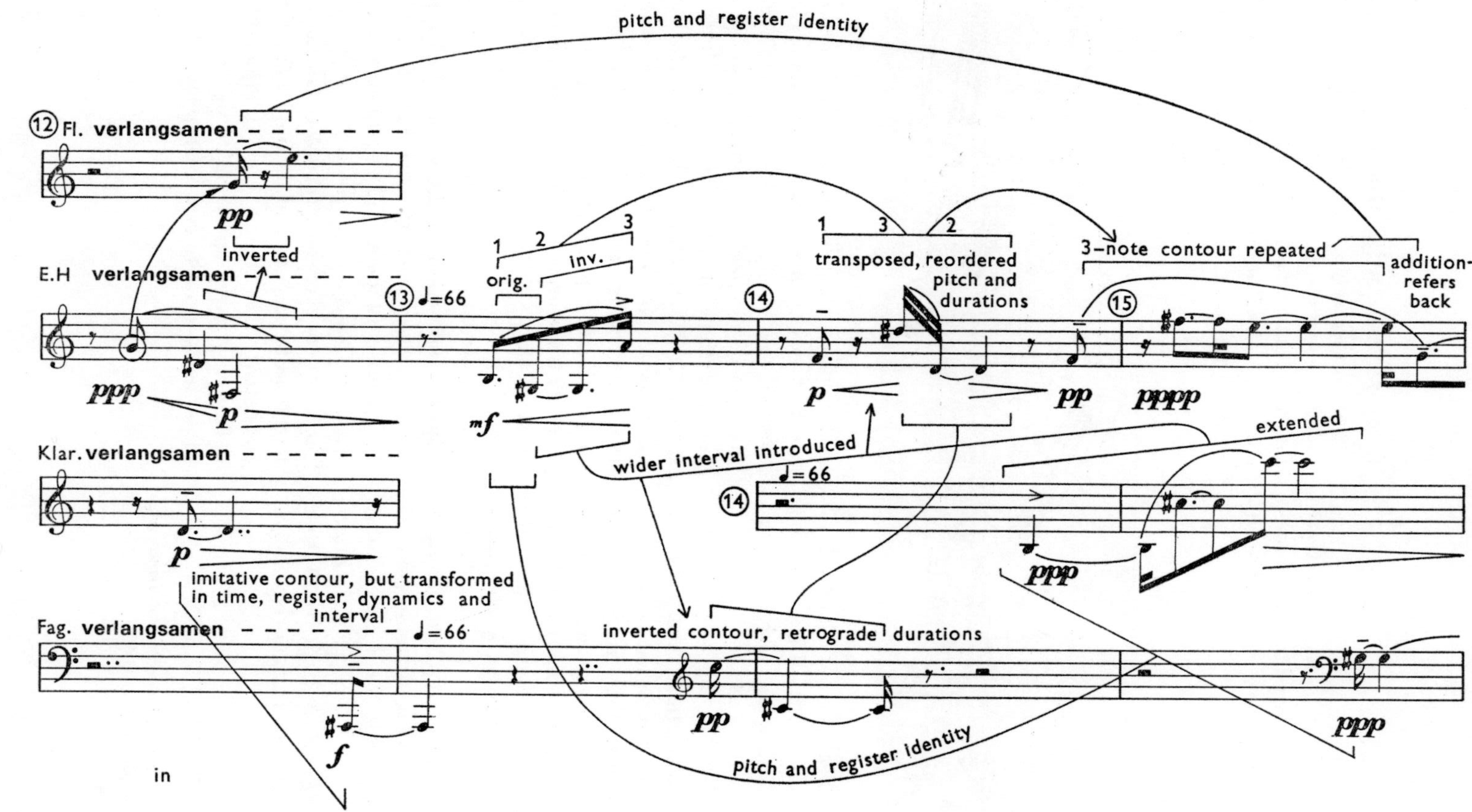
pitch and register identity
⑫ Fl. verlangsamen
pp
inverted
E.H verlangsamen
ppp
p
⑬ ♩=66
1 2 3
orig.
inv.
mf
⑭
1 3 2
transposed, reordered
pitch and
durations
p
pp
3-note contour repeated
addition-
refers
back
⑮
pppp
extended
wider interval introduced
Klar. verlangsamen
p
⑭ ♩=66
ppp
imitative contour, but transformed
in time, register, dynamics and
interval
Fag. verlangsamen
♩=66
f
inverted contour, retrograde durations
pp
ppp
pitch and register identity
in

Ex. 20

beschleunigen - - - - - - verlangsamen - -
Ob.
beschleunigen - - - - - - verlangsamen - -
Fl.
deutliche Lautstärkeunterschiede der Gruppen
beschleunigen - - - - - - verlangsamen - -
Klar.
- - - - - - - - - im Tempo verlangsamen - - - - - /im Tempo
Ob.
- - - - - - - - - im Tempo verlangsamen - - - - - /im Tempo
Fl.
- - - - - - - - - im Tempo verlangsamen - - - - - /im Tempo
Klar.

Ex. 21 *from* 'Oiseaux exotiques' (1955–6) O. Messiaen

7
Gruppen

Gruppen (or in English, 'Groups') for three orchestras was written in two stages. The pitch and tempo sets, the pitch range of each group, a precise rhythmic scheme for the opening of the work and a demonstration of the way orchestras overlap were all planned out in July and August of 1955 in Paspels bei Chur, Switzerland (well before *Zeitmasze* was finished). Stockhausen has sometimes stopped and released a piece for performance at roughly this stage of determinacy; here, during all of 1957 in Cologne, he wrote it out in full detail with nothing left to chance, no imprecise rhythms or approximate pitches. It has often been said that at about this point in musical history the great sham of ferociously complex-looking scores was finally exposed by the fact that some of the composers who wrote them changed with apparent complacency from almost inhuman precision to aleatoric 'chance' techniques, where a good deal 'doesn't matter' as long as it sounds nice and complex. This ferociously complex-looking score alone disposes of that exposure. For all the difficulties and unrealities of the detailed realisation, *Gruppen* always sounds considered and even important, in the sense of having a lot to say both locally and totally; in short, much better than any of the aleatoric scores which were supposed, depending upon your critical outlook, either to supersede it or to prove the vapidity of the whole lot of them.

In discussing the music let me follow Stockhausen's schedule and first say something about the preliminary stage of planning. A body of 109 players is divided into three equal orchestras with the comparatively conventional component families which are situated on three sides of a hall. Thus was reborn instrumental spatial music, the equivalent of the widely spaced loudspeakers in *Gesang der Jünglinge* (composed in the middle of the composition of *Gruppen*), and a continuation of such works as Giovanni Gabrieli's antiphonal works for St. Mark's Venice, Berlioz's *Requiem*, the four spatial levels in 'The Temple of the Grail' music of *Parsifal*, *Die Jakobsleiter*, etc. As Schoenberg picturesquely wrote of the projected end of his *Jakobsleiter*, 'music is streaming in from all sides of the hall'. Schoenberg was also envisaging four spatially separated ensembles – two at different heights, and two at different distances – but in addition to the main ensemble. This was about 1917, but in 1944 he foreshadowed another Stockhausen *idée fixe* by suggesting that the effect could be better achieved by microphones and well-distributed loudspeakers. Stockhausen's thinking on spatial music may well date from Pierre Schaeffer's Paris concerts of 1951–2 in which his group (the one Stockhausen also worked with) composed tapes for three spatially mobile circuits of sound. *Son et Lumière* and stereophonic cinerama also date from the same time. It is interesting that Stockhausen's first sketches for *Gruppen* include parts for loudspeakers – an idea he kept for later use, as was also the idea to have 'free' tempi in the manner of *Zeitmasze*.

The use of a spatial dimension has not only the obvious dramatic justification, but also a structural one. If, for example, a flute is playing B *piano* in orchestra I, and another flute plays A in orchestra III, and then the first flute plays an A and the second flute a B, the listener will be able to separate the lines because they are 'over there' and 'over *there*' as well as 'played by a flute', '*piano*', etc. Thus two arguments can be perceived in a situation where otherwise only one would have been perceptible. In this work Stockhausen is able to use three arguments at once, though he seems to prefer 'fusion' as often as 'counterpoint', throwing tempo-textures around the hall rather than ideas with a more separable identity. More of that later.

The work consists of 174 'groups', each one lasting on average a few seconds and being distributed around one orchestra or another or, more occasionally, two or three at once. Also, for much of the time different groups will overlap, one starting in one orchestra before the previous group has finished in another orchestra. Because nearly every group has a different tempo marking one frequently gets three tempi occurring simultaneously (achieved by having three conductors for the orchestras who have to synchronise with each other and pick up special sound cues from other orchestras).

The tempi are chosen from the 'chromatic' scale (the steps of the scale 'to be sensed as equally large') between ♩ = 60 and ♩ = 120. Double speeds – metronome markings times two – are used intermittently as well. These tempi are ordered serially. This is the moment to introduce the set of the work, as it influences almost everything that was planned after this point:

Ex. 22

There are four points about this particular set. 1. It is degenerate; the second hexachord (6 notes) is a retrograde of the first, so by transposing the set six semitones higher (T^6) you re-duplicate T^0 backwards,

Ex. 23
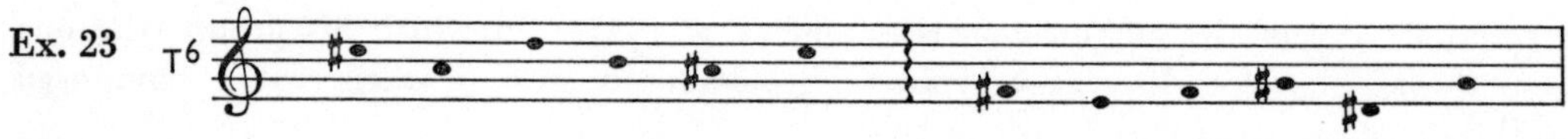

thus cutting down the field of possible forms and, more important here, of different transpositional *levels* from twelve to six (a level is a transposition of the set which may be played forwards or backwards, or both or with certain segments retraced or jumbled, as so often happens in this work). Forwards and backwards are recognisably the same thing, therefore: a fact that will be seen to be important later.
2. It is an all-interval set, which means that it contains all eleven intervals once each. This is useful in that every interval in the work is 'related' to the set, however incidentally and decoratively it may appear, but backfires into one of the most important deficiencies of the work (deliberate no doubt on Stockhausen's part, but which nevertheless I feel rather strongly), the deficiency of motivic purposefulness – 'motivic' in the very widest sense.
3. Each of the two hexachords is half of the chromatic scale (cf. *Piano Piece I* amongst others, for unordered chromatic hexachords) thus giving Stockhausen a background for his clusters.
4. A negative point. It is a first order all-combinatorial set, in other words a rather special one that could be combined with different forms of itself to make many-dimensional structures. Stockhausen is not interested in this or did not know about it; in this sense at least, his thinking is less developed than Schoenberg's or Webern's, not to mention what Babbitt was doing seven years previously in this dimension and in rhythm as well.

In the application of the set to rhythm Stockhausen and Messiaen in *Mode de Valeurs et d'Intensités* and Boulez in *Structures* go beyond the pointers laid by the Second Viennese School (but not beyond Babbitt who antedates them too), though whether this application is valid has been much disputed. In general in the Darmstadt School, total serialism led to some things of value, but not entirely the expected ones. A new type of perpetual change over a scale or ladder of elements was born that gave rise to a different type of sound in which constant surprises were found rather than constant logic.

Here is a plan of the tempi. I have taken G to equal ♩= 120; but I could have started on any other note as far as the tempo proportions one to another are concerned. If G = (♩ = 60), then G sharp = (♩ = 63·5), A = (♩ = 67), A sharp = (♩ = 71) etc. → G = (♩ = 120) (Ex. 24).

There are twelve sets at five out of a possible six transpositional levels, though the last is an aggregate of the twelve notes rather than an ordered set. There are no inversions, only retrogrades. (Likewise there are no extended inversions in the pitch structure until just before the end, at group 158.)

These sets do not necessarily start with the first note of the set, but permutate the starting point (as, again, in the pitch structure); and the intervals across the sets, from twelfth note to first note, are the same procession of intervals as is offered by the set itself. The sign [indicates the set starting point. Example 25 shows how this permutational scheme is distributed.*

The glissando notes represent passages of continuously fluctuating tempo of which the

* I am indebted to Gottfried Michael Koenig's diagram in *Die Reihe*, vol. 8, pp. 92–3, for the preparation of certain aspects of my example 25.

Ex. 24

Aggregate: 1
Beginning with group: 1
2
14
3
33
4
45
5
58
6
77
7
89
8
100
9
113
10
135
11
149
12
162

Ex. 25

= orch. 1 = orch. 1+2
= orch. 2
= orch. 3 = tutti

Tempi expressed as pitch:

Group: (1) (2) (3) (4) (5) (6) (7) (8) (9) (10)

Interval ratios:
10 : 8 12 : 5 7 : 2 2 : 7
3 : 4 6 : 11 9 : 13 11 :

Metronomic tempi: ♩ = 120 95 127 107 101 113.5 80 71

Type of unit or fundamental pulse:

(11) (12) (13) (14) (15) (16) (17) (18) (19) (20) (21) (22)

Violin solos

5 : 12 8 : 10 9 : 10
6 4 : 3 10 : 8 11 :
75.5 90 67 85 67 75.5

(23) (24) (25) (26)(27)(28) (29) (30) (31) (32) (33) (34) (35) (36) (37) (38)

4 : 7 10 : 3 2 : 5 5 : 2 7 : 12 6 : 11 7 : 5 11 : 3
8 6 : 13 12 : 9 8 : 11 3 : 8 3 : 4 8 : 9 9 : 8 10 :
107 95 101 120 90 113.5 80 63.5 85 71 95 90 101 71 63.5 67

written as 120

(39) (40) (41) (42) (43) (44) (45) (46) (47)(48)(49) (50) (51) (52) (53) (54)

('wrong order')

4 : 6 5 : 7 12 : 4 9 : 13 6 : 8 3 : 11 13 : 9 11 :
12 13 : 4 2 : 13 12 : 5 5 : 2 12 : 10 7 : 4 2 : 7
80 120 75.5 107 85 113.5 95 67 107 71 60 113.5 63.5 90 80

(55) (56) (57) (58) (59) (60) (61) (62) (63) (64) (65) (66) (67) (68) (69)

6 4 : 3 3 : 10 7 : 4 10 : 9 12 : 7 2 : 5 5 : 2
10 : 12 6 : 11 13 : 6 11 : 8 8 6 : 13 4 : 3 8 : 11 7 :
85 101 75.5 71 120 113.5 63.5 90 80 85 101 75.5 95 67 107

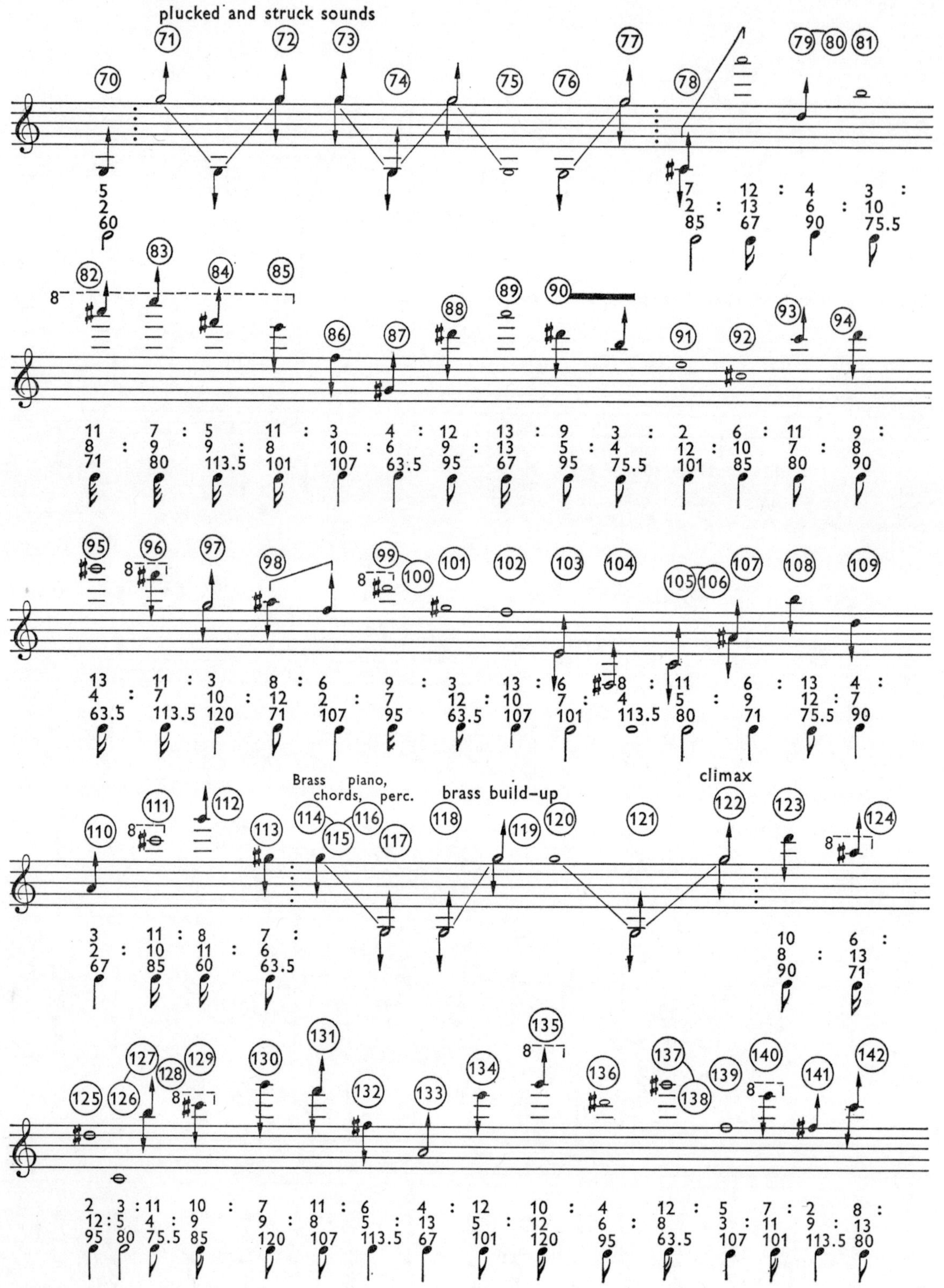
plucked and struck sounds
Brass piano,
chords, perc.
brass build-up
climax

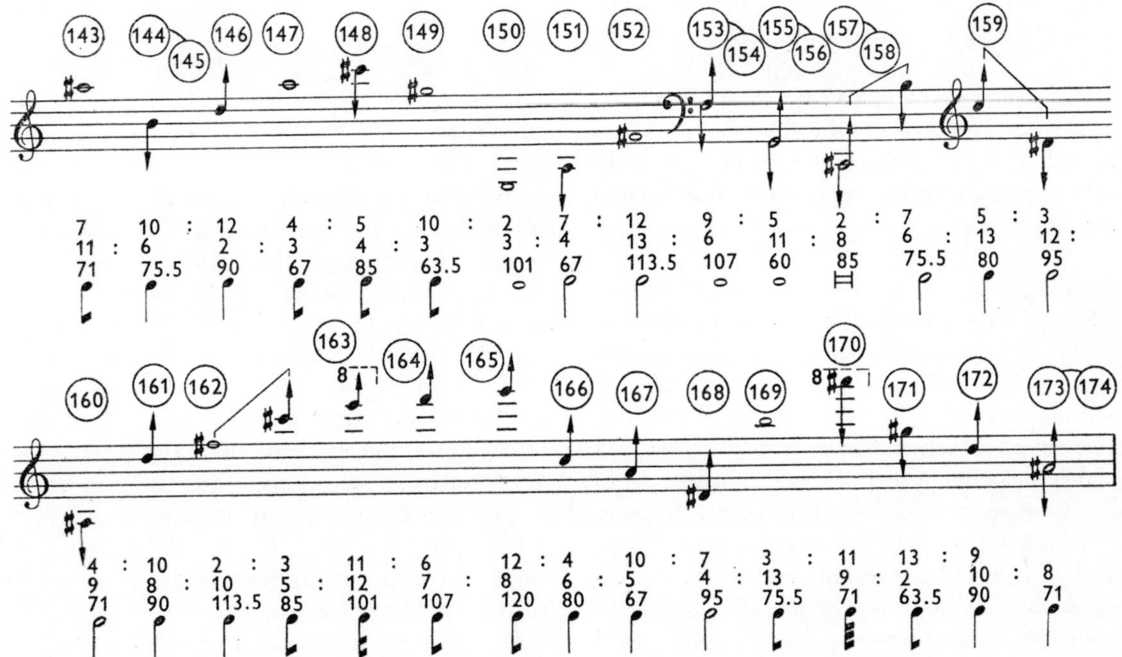

printed notes are only the starting or finishing points and therefore no more important than all the points in between (represented by a line here, and by accelerando or ritardando in the score). Therefore they are not counted in the serial scheme as they include all notes; they act as three big interludes. I shall call them 'interludes', which is strictly correct, though this term must not be taken to imply that they are less emphasised in the structure, for the contrary is the case. They are quite distinct in character from the other sections. The first (groups 16–22) is dominated by a solo violin line shared out between the leaders of the three orchestras, accompanied mostly by trichords (derived three-note segments sounded as chords). The second (71–76) is a passage of plucked and struck sounds culminating at group 77 in an orgy of sounds marked *fff* (*klingen lassen*) – 'allow to reverberate'. The third (114–122) forms the climax of the work. It falls into five subdivisions: first, brass calls 'set the wild echoes flying', muted (distant) and unmuted; secondly sustained brass hexachords whirl continuously round in space; thirdly the piano plays a cadenza as the brass hexachords fade into the distant haze; fourthly the percussion from all three orchestras build up (crescendo and accelerando) on skin and metal instruments; and finally the full brass and percussion join in the long climactic section, one of the densest climaxes in modern music.

There is one other group which perhaps falls into this category, it is a serially created 'gap', and so it is without tempo rather than in fluctuating tempo. It is group eight, and it consists of clusters whose component notes are released successively, with the top note singled out dynamically and timbrally. It is likewise a complete break with what happens on either side and has a rather special role that I shall explain later.

Looking at Example 24 one might be forgiven for expecting strong articulations to occur at groups fourteen, thirty-three, forty-five, fifty-eight etc., or perhaps at the initial note of each set shape within the permutation. But there are no such articulations, not even at 135 which looks like a sort of recapitulation. As in this case, so with many of the others, the start of a new set is merely a continuation group, part of something previous and relatively insignificant. Even if Stockhausen did demarcate the beginnings of sets two more factors would militate against a satisfying serial experience of hearing the same tempo intervals pass over and over again. First, the exact tempo is often hard to hear in any individual group, such are the complexities of off-the-beat accentuation, and secondly it is extremely hard for conductors (and listeners) to gauge these differences in tempo to the precision necessary for distinguishing whether the new tempo is, say, a perfect fifth or a minor sixth faster than the old tempo – serially a matter of vital importance. The Tempo Plan, then, for all its striking originality remains something of a background prop whose main function is to give variety-within-limits rather than a real experience of form in the macrocosm.

A plan of the starting times and durations of the groups must have been planned on the same drawing board as the tempo plan, for as Stockhausen explains in his article '. . . how time passes . . .' they are both part of an all-embracing temporal scheme. The way he arrived at group starting times and durations* is very involved indeed. Stockhausen's tempi, if you read along the ♩ = line of Example 25, are all between 60 and 120, i.e. in one 'octave'. This is merely for conducting convenience. He makes octave transpositions of the tempi by using different notational units as the fundamental pulse, as set out in the unit line of the example, and the pitches in that chart are placed according to these various octave transpositions, high for the demisemiquavers (= fast), low for the breves (= slow). So much for the real tempo, as opposed to the conductor's beat.

In order to make the relative lengths of the groups one to another serial, Stockhausen takes the intervals from one tempo to the next, approximated by the numbers in the 'Intervals' rows,† and uses the second number in each ratio to determine the number of those units-at-that-tempo of which the group will consist. Thus the second group has 8 × 𝅗𝅥, the third 4 × 𝅗𝅥, the fourth 5 × 𝅝, the fifth 11 × 𝅗𝅥, the sixth 2 × 𝅜 and so on. In other words, if the third group is $\frac{4}{3}$ as fast as the second, the first three minims of the second group must equal the component four minims of the third group, and group 3, or

* See account of it in '. . . how time passes . . .', *Die Reihe*, vol. 3, pp. 21–6.

† These interval ratios can be worked out by comparing frequencies, i.e. if the first note, G, equals 392 Hz., and the next, D sharp, equals 313 Hz., one quickly sees that the first number is $\frac{10}{8}$ of the second.

every group is therefore required to wait its own duration (counting from the beginning of the previous group) before entering with music of exactly that duration, because both sides of a ratio are, of course, equal. The first number of the ratio represents units of rests in the old tempo, the second number represents units of music in the new tempo. This seems quite a realistic musical plan despite its conceptual complexity, certainly compared, say, with Berg's numerology in the *Lyric Suite* or *Lulu*, or for that matter, much Medieval and Renaissance thought.*

Let us now pass to the second stage of composition, the detailed realisation of the general plan.

The most general remarks that can be made concerning the make-up of the average group are that *pitch-wise* it is often limited to fixed pitches, i.e. notes stick in the same octave disposition, giving a more or less static feeling, and *rhythm-wise* it consists of a fundamental duration, usually the bar, subdivided into 2, 3, 4, 5, 6, 7, 8, 9, 10, 11, 12, etc., or a selection of these quicker subdivisions. We should examine both these characteristics in more detail.

* See, for instance, M. van Crevel's article on his transcription of the fifteenth-century mass, *Missa Sub Tuum Praesidium* by Jacob Obrecht into modern proportional notation. Dr. van Crevel discovered simple relations between the durations of various portions of the mass, and between the pitch and duration of the individual notes. M. van Crevel, 'Structururgeheimen bÿ Obrecht' in *Tÿdschrift Der Vereniging Voor Nederlandse Muziekgescheidenis*, vol. XIX (1960–1), p. 87.

First, the fixed pitches. Stockhausen uses, as another serial ordering principle, different band widths for each of the groups. He obtains widths by reading Example 25 in retrograde, taking the serial procession of *intervals* proffered and making them equal the span between the extreme outer notes of the band widths. He places these bands below the note on the chart.* The 'interludes' are not confined to band widths since they are outside the tempo plan. This is a concept borrowed from the electronic studio where it is strictly used to describe the range of frequencies allowed to come out of a band pass filter. In other words the filter can suppress most of the received sound and select from this total an adjustable band width. It is very typical of an electronic composer to think in these terms and is a good example of the fascinating new vistas opened up in one branch of an art by exploration in another. The experience of spontaneously making mental associations with electronic pieces when listening to instrumental pieces of the avant-garde is now very common, and indicative of the degree to which the cross-fertilisation between the two media (recently considered fundamentally irreconcilable) has been accomplished.

Stockhausen at one extreme uses very narrow band widths where the pitches are obsessively fixed (Ex. 26).

Notice that the only exception, the cluster in the piano, is a cue for conductor III to start beating five silent beats at ♩ = 75·5 before the

* Not, as has been suggested by Gottfried Michael Koenig (*Die Reihe*, vol. 8, p. 94), by positioning the band above or below the note.

Ex. 26

⑩
Kleine Flöte
Almglocken
Triangel
Metall
Klavier
Violinen
Bratschen
hart
normal
sul pont.
gliss.
div.
div. 8
♩=75,5

Ex. 27

108
♩=75,5
ff
f
pp crescendo
Hörner
1.
2.
3.
Trompeten
Metall
weich
Celesta
Harfe
Violinen arco
I
II
III
(♩=71)
Violonen IV 1,2
Bratschen arco
Violoncelli
arco
Kontrabässe

Ex. 28

entry of group 11 – a largely practical device. This sort of group, because of its strong constraints, superimposes effectively and with clarity on other groups.

In other groups he uses wider band widths, in this case a tritone, G sharp → D, the same as in group 1 (Ex. 27).

And as the band widths become wider, the notes need not be so dense (another concept from the electronic studio mentality). For instance, group 143 is built of three notes, G sharp, E, A (the first three of T^{11}), though the E flat clarinet, which has a very special role throughout the piece, is referring to another system (more of that later), and the low brass give a cue to conductor III while referring to the pitches of one group back. When the groups include all twelve pitch classes, it is then possible for Stockhausen to organise them according to the twelve-note set. Group 23, for instance, has a predominant major sixth dense band width F sharp – D sharp with the two notes needed to make up twelve fixed very much higher, separated to refer back to the previous long solo violin passage (Ex. 28).

This group exemplifies the tendency of many of the more complex groups to articulate a set by successive entries in different instruments, and then to double back on these pitches in a

Ex. 29

Ex. 30

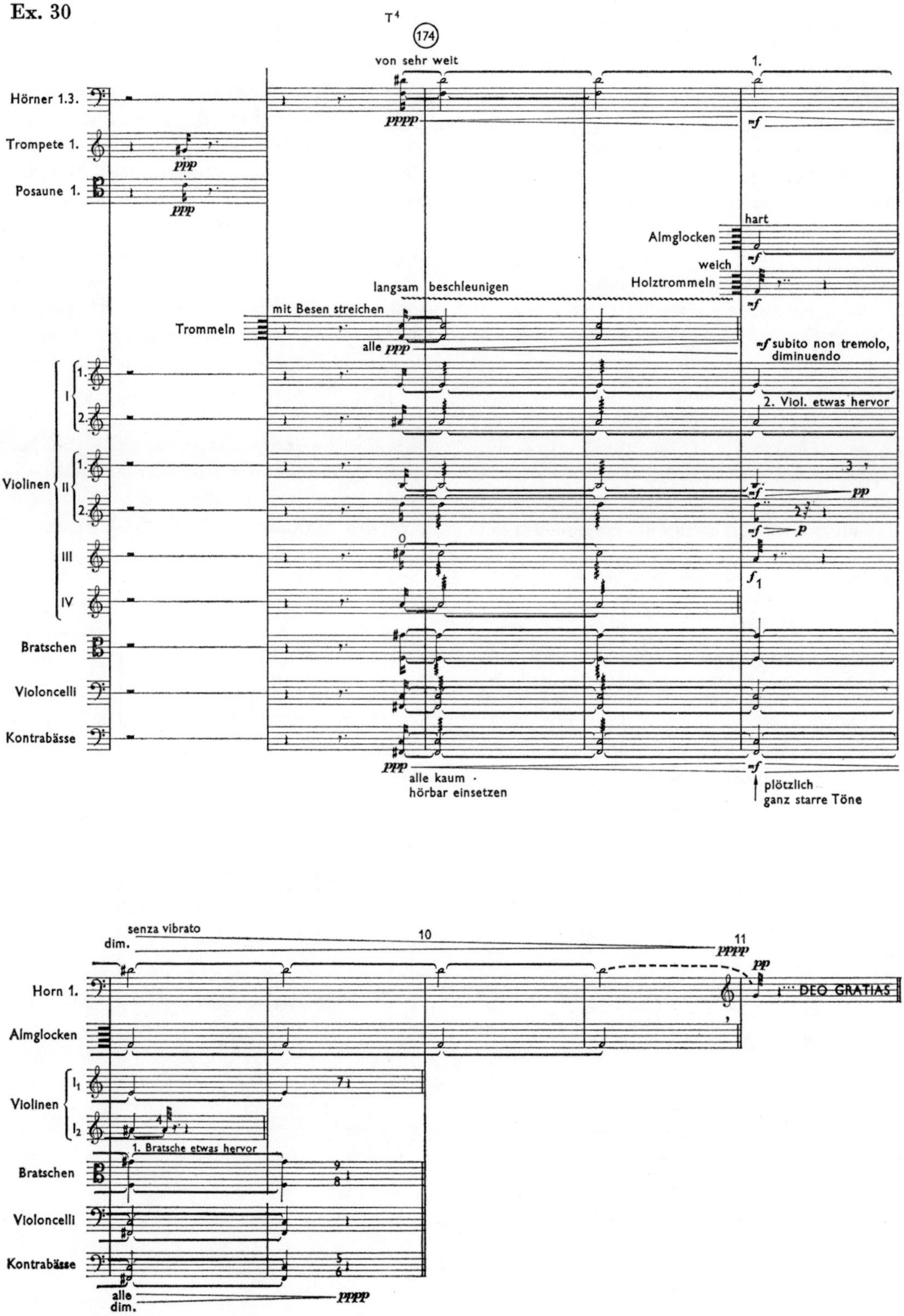

T4
174
von sehr weit
1.
Hörner 1.3.
pppp
mf
Trompete 1.
ppp
Posaune 1.
ppp
hart
Almglocken
mf
weich
Holztrommeln
mf
langsam beschleunigen
mit Besen streichen
Trommeln
alle ppp
mf subito non tremolo, diminuendo
Violinen
I 1.
I 2.
2. Viol. etwas hervor
II 1.
II 2.
mf pp
mf p
III
f
IV
Bratschen
Violoncelli
Kontrabässe
ppp
alle kaum-hörbar einsetzen
mf
plötzlich ganz starre Töne

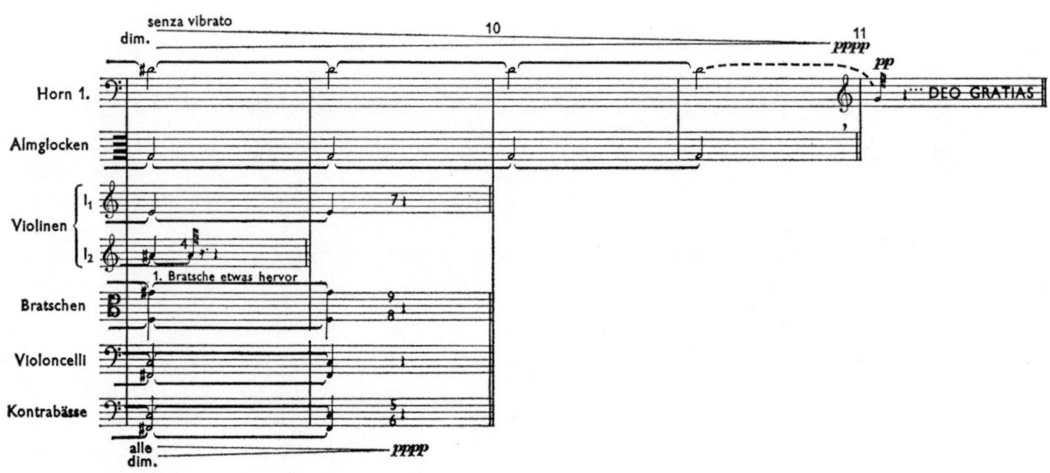

less systematic manner, perhaps suggesting other set segments, such as an inversion in the first half of the second bar.

Or, the serial structure may be more clearly adhered to, as in group 80 (Ex. 29).

Or, as we have seen in earlier works, Stockhausen turns articulation on its head and expresses the set by not-playing it in a set order, i.e. by release points. Several smaller such gestures lead up to the final group in Ex. 30.

Rather more often than not, however, groups have more than twelve fixed pitches and at the very end of the scale, as it were, it no longer makes sense to talk about fixed pitches at all.

Before going on to discuss other pitch arguments, such as melodic form, and then to the big questions of group relationships, I will finish the description of the average group with a look at its rhythmic structure.

Stockhausen says in '. . . how time passes . . .': 'We described the durations in each group as fundamental durations' (that's to say, the various quantities of units or fundamental pulses). 'Now we have to ask what sort of *formant-spectra* these fundamental durations will receive (just as in the case of fundamental tones we had to ask which instrument – which "tone colour", or, better, which *formant-rhythm* – should be linked to the fundamental tones, or which instrument to which fundamental tone). The fact that there are *groups* of fundamental durations means that a formant-spectrum must be related to the supra-ordered duration of the whole group, i.e. to the *group-phase*. The spectrum to be composed is then called a *group-spectrum*.

'The most diverse methods of serial composition can be used in deciding the number (the shorter the fundamental duration, the fewer formants!), the combination, the register (fixed or movable formants), the changes of register(!), the intensity relationships, etc., of the formants. A formant-spectrum will then be seen as a unitary time-complex, characterised by its total duration, envelope-curve, average speed, speed tendency, average intensity, density, density progression, sonority (which group or combination of instruments), sound-form, movement in pitch, harmonic field, and so on. The resultant of all these compositional details is what we have described generally as the formant-rhythm (instead of the notion of "tone-colour"), and this will be heard as either the *rhythm of the sound* or the *rhythm of the bar*, depending on whether it has to do with pitch or duration.'*

An example that Stockhausen gives of a seven-bar group-spectrum is shown in Ex. 31.

It is a picture of group 7 with two interrupting almost silent bars left out of the middle. One or two inaccuracies have inexplicably crept in between the score and this diagram as the reader will see if he compares the next example with the diagram. It is the fourth bar of the diagram and contains divisions of the fundamental semibreve pulse into up to twenty-six 'formants'. Actually it is the most complex bar of the work by quite a long chalk in this respect (Ex. 32).

---

* *Die Reihe*, vol. 3, pp. 25–6.

Ex. 31

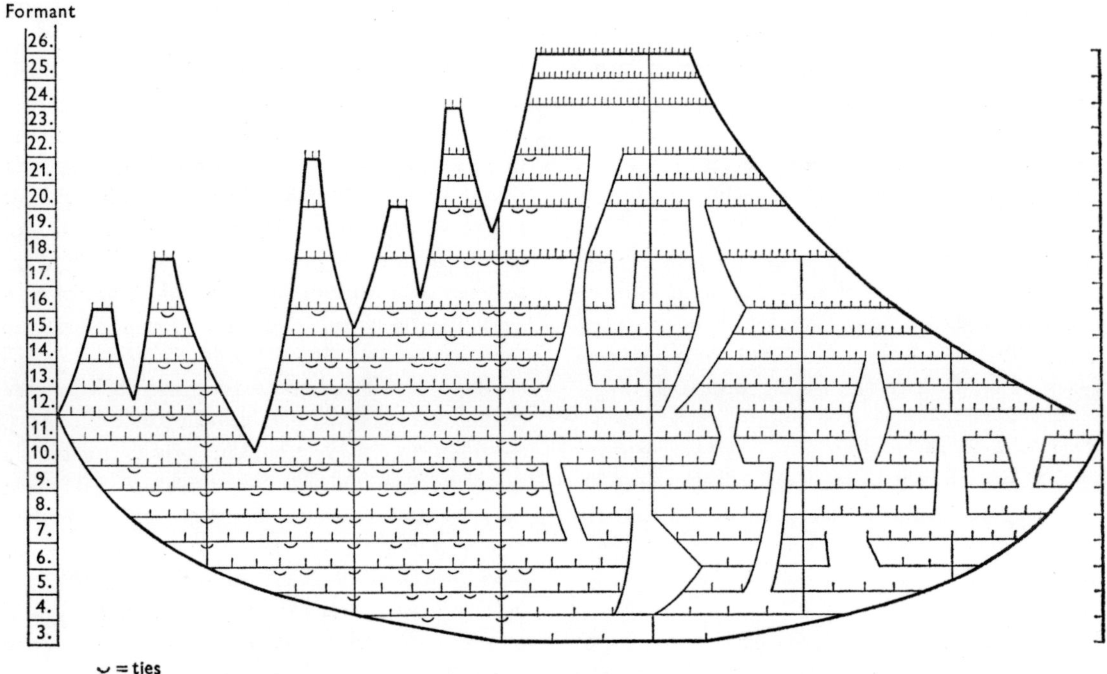
Formant
26.
25.
24.
23.
22.
21.
20.
19.
18.
17.
16.
15.
14.
13.
12.
11.
10.
9.
8.
7.
6.
5.
4.
3.
⌣ = ties

Ex. 32

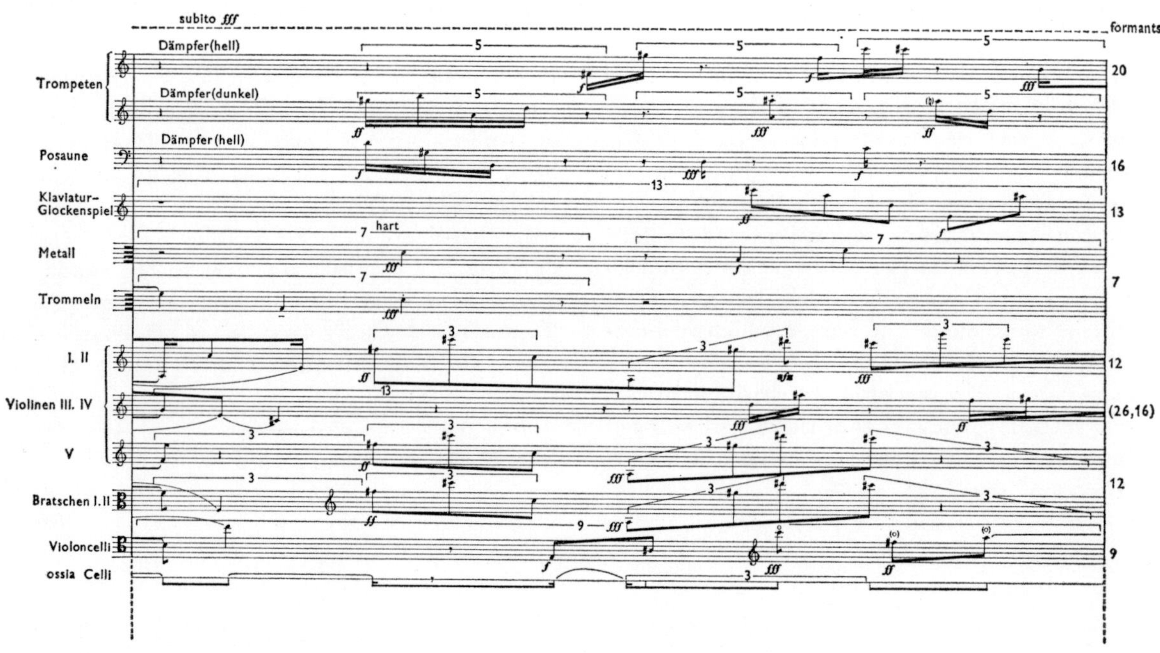
subito fff
formants
Trompeten
Dämpfer(hell)
Dämpfer(dunkel)
Posaune
Dämpfer (hell)
Klaviatur-Glockenspiel
Metall
hart
Trommeln
I. II
Violinen III. IV
V
Bratschen I. II
Violoncelli
ossia Celli
20
16
13
7
12
(26,16)
12
9

Ex. 32 (cont'd)

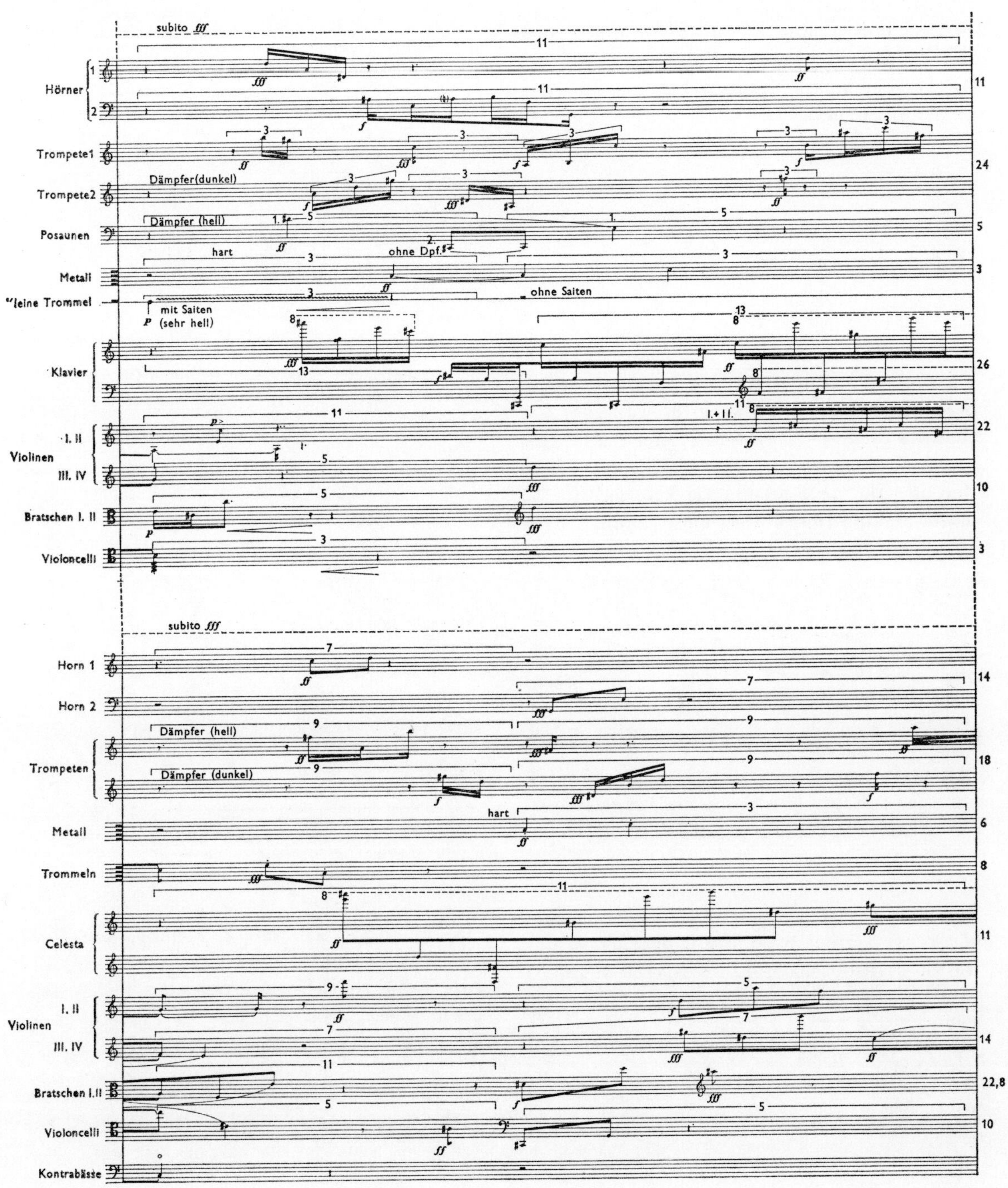
subito fff
Hörner
Trompete1
Dämpfer(dunkel)
Trompete2
Dämpfer (hell)
Posaunen
hart
ohne Dpf.
Metall
leine Trommel
mit Saiten
(sehr hell)
ohne Saiten
Klavier
I. II
Violinen
III. IV
I.+II.
Bratschen I. II
Violoncelli
subito fff
Horn 1
Horn 2
Dämpfer (hell)
Trompeten
Dämpfer (dunkel)
hart
Metall
Trommeln
Celesta
I. II
Violinen
III. IV
Bratschen I. II
Violoncelli
Kontrabässe
11
24
5
3
26
22
10
3
14
18
6
8
11
14
22,8
10

Koenig has shown* that the *number* of component formants or subdivisions of a fundamental pulse going on in any group is also determined in relation to the set. So, for instance, as in the middle of the set (in close spacing) we have

Ex. 33

so it seems reasonable that a group that has 3 formants will be succeeded by one that has the smallest interval (i.e. 1) of formants *less* than its predecessor, making 2 formants; this group likewise will be succeeded by a group that has the next-to-smallest interval (i.e. 2) more, making that a 4-formant group.

Ex. 34

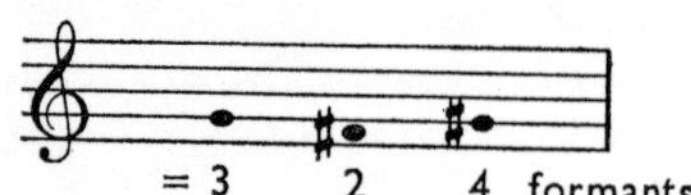

In certain places, as a variation, Stockhausen has the formants of a group occurring successively instead of simultaneously (Ex. 35).

This is only a tiny sample of something that occurs on a larger scale, but it does show how the subdivisions have intervals related to the

Ex. 35

sets. If 3 = D sharp, then

Ex. 36

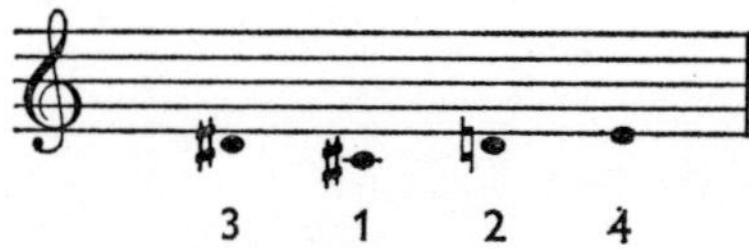

Having given the reader, I hope, a general idea of the structure of groups, now I will discuss some of the ways the more prominent linear ideas and arguments are shaped. There are several types of linear set-expression.

The first, which has already been touched on, is the procession of band widths through the

* Koenig, *Die Reihe*, vol. 8, p. 95.

tempo plan read backwards. This can give an audible top fixed pitch, which Stockhausen sometimes brings out by instrumentation and dynamics. See, for instance, groups 123–134, which correspond to the 'pitches' of groups 56–45 reading backwards on Example 25. The clusters which characterise the section articulate the whole band width clearly too. Note that groups 126 and 127 have the same tempo, and therefore the same band width. Also note that a band width is only a *predominant* structure. Fantasy weaves many little strands outside its range.

A second type of linear construction springs out of this. As the top notes of the band width succession are slowly unfolding a set, the groups themselves may sew on top of that set the same set more quickly as a group structure. For instance, group 141 has the band width

Ex. 37

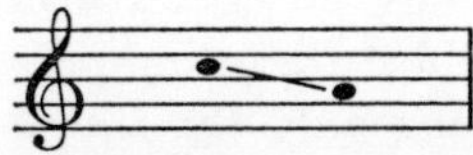

as found between the tempi of groups 38 and 39.* At this point the band widths are proceeding through the third aggregate of Example 25 backwards (T^4) and the marimbaphone quickly takes the C and A five notes further into T^4.

* There is an inexplicable double tempo in group 39 wherein the serial order is reversed. It is the only such re-ordering in the piece, and the fact that Stockhausen treats the band width as if there had been no re-ordering indicates that 'artistic license' was taken.

Ex. 38

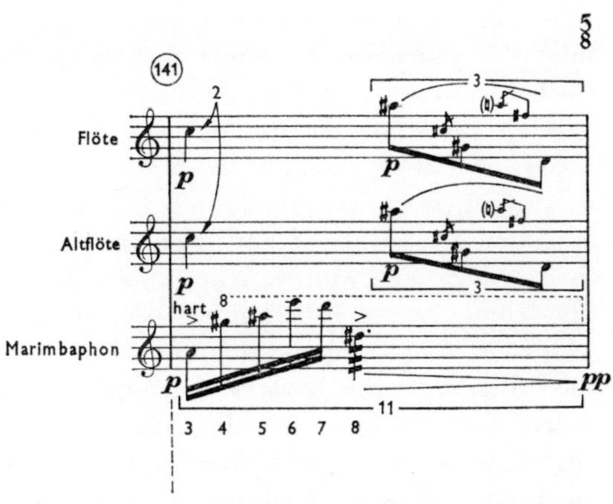

A third type is constructed from the pitches of Example 25 in retrograde, as with the band width sequence, and yet is independent of it. Stockhausen goes through the chart making these notes prominent in sound and in the score, drawing rings around them to make sure the conductors articulate them clearly, so that the result is a sort of cantus firmus. It all starts off in group 8, a non-rhythmic interlude group, where not only are the first seven notes of the retrograded tempo plan displayed in recitative style in their 'correct' octave dispositions, but also the first seven band widths, whose top notes are of course the same ones, are recapitulated and linked with them. It is as if we are being shown how to hear the piece. If we did not give aural importance to the top notes of the first seven band widths, or wondered where the band widths came from, Stockhausen tells us in group 8 that the top notes *are* the structure and the procession of band widths is determined by them and their intervals. (As always with Stockhausen, the system is not the whole story. Just after the sixth cluster in group 8 there occurs a quite solo *ff* C sharp in the violin up above the cluster's range; in fact at the pitch of the C sharp in the final aggregate of Example 25. It *is* part of that scheme, but the F sharp and D only occur (as outsiders) in group 11, similarly indicated by an arrow and accompanied by their proper band widths. When this C sharp's turn comes round in the procession of band widths it is omitted, presumably because of the subordinate role it plays in group 162 as a *tempo*! But Stockhausen did not wish the aggregate of top notes of band widths to be incomplete, so, with an admirable sense for the exigencies of order, he put it in as 'counterpoint' in group 8 and gave it a sequel in group 11.)

Other types of cantus firmus used are: long, sustained pedals (groups 40–57, T^1 or retrograde of ninth aggregate); timbral and dynamic articulation (groups 145–153, orchestra II vibraphone *sfz*, T^{10}); and articulation by style (groups 156–161, the set passed round the orchestras tremolo or flutter-tongue, T^{11} or the second aggregate in retrograde).

I mentioned earlier the special role of the E flat clarinet. It is a sort of herald who announces in shrill tones every now and again throughout the piece one set only – T^{10} – two notes at a time. The close spacing of this instrument's set in the highest register *ff* makes for a comparatively easily followable statement. It plays virtually no other loud notes. This list of its dramatic appearances will show all that needs to be said of the little irregularities that occur:

Group	T^{10} (order numbers)
24	0, 1
36	1, 2
46	2, 3
62	3, 4
(76 ↓	1, 2, 7, 8 (0, 1, 2, 3, 4), 5, 6, 7, 8, 9, 10, 11 (flute and oboe also))
77	4, 5
(81	7, 5, 6)
90	6, 7, 8 (part of a T^{10} texture)
106	7, 8
123	8
142	9, 10
156	10, 11
168	11, 0

Finally on linear serialism, a word about 'multiple functions'; that's when one note belongs to two sets at the same time. They occur a lot in Schoenberg, in the Orchestral Variations, for instance, where the theme is often a cantus firmus which systematically generates other sets off its long body; it is a stock technique of which Stockhausen is using only the simpler aspects. Groups 165 to the end illustrate the ending of the final cantus firmus composed of the first aggregate in retrograde (see Example 25). This cantus is played by bells or piano plus soft tremolo after-echoes, and the same notes do for the cantus and the start of another set in the 'accompaniment'. There is no 11th note of T^6, however, until the final group 174 goes through all of T^6 and finishes itself, the work *and* the cantus off with the final solo horn grace note (cf. Example 30).

Needless to say, there are many smaller linear set expressions which do not come under the

Gruppen

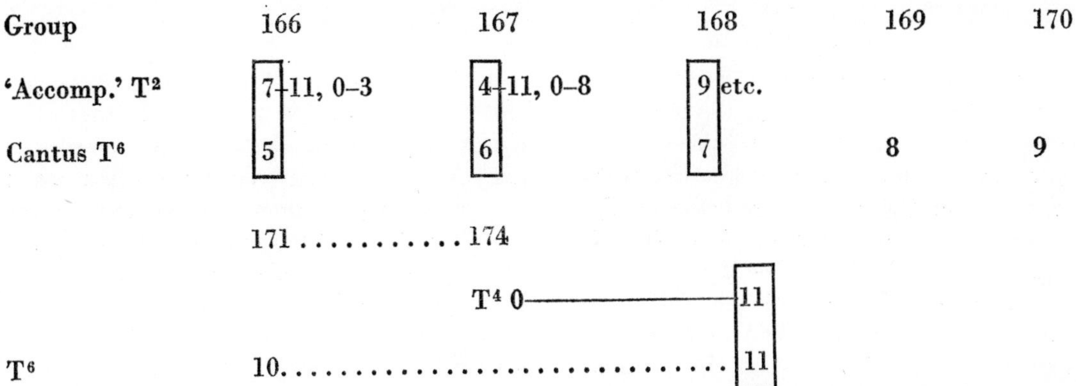

heading of cantus firmus but which perform the tying together operations within single groups. I have already given one or two examples of them, and since they are fairly simple and traditional, in so far as such an élitist procedure as serialism can be so called, I won't go into them further.

It now remains to give a few indications of group inter-relationships and characters. This concerns the surface of the structure which is very easy to hear, i.e. that one group is loud and therefore contrasts with the next that is soft, and so I shall leave most of the perceiving to the listener and only add a few hints. There are, as in all Stockhausen works, several dimensions in which there is a range of change between two extremes. Isolation → Fusion is a very obvious one in this work where spatial separation is used, and Similarity → Contrast another, because the work is orchestral and can therefore present an enormous palette of timbral, figurational, textural and rhythmic identities (soloistic → (chamber music) → orchestral), though of course the number of formants used (as opposed to how they are used) is serially controlled. It would be tedious to list a description of these identities; rather more interesting is to note how identities slowly grow across the groups. For instance, the climax of the work in group 122 is the blossoming of a steady growth in brass and piano sounds, which occur from group 78 on, that is to say, throughout the whole of the main-structure section between the middle and final interludes. See especially group 86 (muted dense chords), group 91 (piano solo), 97 (low brass staccato), 101 (muted chord under piano solo), 102 (brass figures), and then the gradual build-up in the interlude itself of staccato figures and held hexachords (at group 116), all of which identities are going to become at the climax the most memorable (that is, have the strongest identities) of the work.

An example of a large scale modulation (electronic usage again) of sound occurs after the cantus firmus previously described as 'timbral and dynamic, groups 145–153 in the orchestra II vibraphone *sfz*'. As the sharp notes of the vibraphone (without vibrato) are finishing in group 154, they are taken over by the woody marimbaphone I, and in group 155 by wood drums, or African slotted drums, in all three orchestras, thus scattering and diffusing the sound into indefinite pitch. This modulation is now developed in group 156 by having quick grace note figures rotate around three duets: wood drums and marimbaphone in orchestra I, wood drums and vibraphone (as before) in II, and wood drums and marimbaphone in III. The next group adds a keyboard instrument to each duet – a keyboard glockenspiel, a piano and a celesta respectively, and then, having reached its full size of three trios, this particular growth begins magically to burst open, disseminating its seeds into other structures, its wood sounds slowly decreasing in frequency and its grace notes transferring themselves to woodwind instruments – grace notes having scarcely occurred in the score before here being therefore very noticeable. This occurs in groups 159, 161 and 162.

Finally, a word about densities of chords. In the interlude sections, where a band width is not in operation, Stockhausen uses his *Piano Piece X* technique of keeping the number of parts in a chord consistent, to give a uniform density. In the first interlude, for instance, strings of three-part chords, punctuated by several isolated five-part chords, get more and more contrapuntal until they become six-part chords just before the change to chamber music texture at group 21. The remainder of the section is founded on spatially diminuendoing four-part chords.

Even the vicious density of group 122, the brass and percussion climax, is a carefully ordered progression of chord densities. It consists of fragmentary lines of a few notes length which are 'harmonised' note for note in five parts at first, then in four, then in three and finally in six and seven. Naturally there is a big rhythmic change between the texture of many thin three-part lines and the texture of few thick six-part lines. At the end of the group the six- or seven-part lines tend to play in rhythmic unison, thus making twelve- or more part chords. The changes within this magnificent riot of a group are quite possible to perceive on repeated hearings.

Gruppen is a paradoxical work; it is possibly the most involved of European total serial works, and yet there is an enormous amount of freedom in the details. There is a vast theory constructed almost 'outside' the work which must have taken a truly Joyceian fanaticism to write out, yet the parts in which Stockhausen is being most himself and at his best are those in which the theory has least influence, i.e. the interludes and the pitch structures of the final sections, structures not directed quite so much by band width clusters as elsewhere in the piece. The band width system is very original, though there is a kind of conceptual precedent in Bartók, who uses an equally systematic, if simpler, procedure, with golden section band widths based on the Fibonacci series – 3, 5, 8, 13 etc. semitones wide.* Indeed there is much in the more systematic aspects of the piece that is extremely effective, but there is also some of which the point, at present at least, is still difficult to hear.

---

* See the article by Ernö Lendvai in *Module, Symmetry, Proportion*, edited by Gyorgy Kepes, Studio Vista, London, 1966.

8

Piano Piece XI and Gesang der Jünglinge

Yet another piece to be composed in 1956, this most amazingly inventive and fertile patch of Stockhausen's creative life so far, is *Piano Piece XI*. And there is one more too – *Gesang der Jünglinge* (1955–6). As *Piano Piece XI* is next on the opus list, Nr. 7, I will make a few comments on it first. Its revolutionary format is fairly well known by now. Briefly, it consists of 19 length-related groups of notes distributed in random formation on a sheet of paper. The performer looks 'at random and begins with any group, the first that catches his eye; this he plays, choosing for himself tempo (small notes always excepted), dynamic level and type of attack. At the end of the first group he reads the tempo, dynamic and attack indications that follow (there is a scale of six for each), and looks at random to any other group, which he then plays in accordance with the latter indications. . . . When a group is arrived at for the second time, directions in brackets become valid; these are mainly transpositions to the first or second octave up or down . . . notes are also added or omitted. When a group is arrived at for the third time, one possible realisation of the piece is completed. This being so, it may come about that certain groups are played once only or not at all. This *Piano Piece* should if possible be performed twice or more in the course of a programme.' (From performer's note on the score.)

The variable order and modes of performance are, of course, the most striking aspect of this work joining it to the company of 'mobiles' by composers as far apart as Earle Brown and Boulez, though the former, inspired by the 'mobiles' of the sculptor Alexander Calder, was in the field well before *Piano Piece XI*. The really important points about this type of composition are twofold: the last sentence of the quotation is significant, and Stockhausen says, 'The field structure of a large form like this will become clearer, naturally . . . when it is played several times in succession'; and only when one has heard enough of the possible versions to gain an idea of the total musical space can one see the background against which a selection (which has a certain field-size) is displayed. In Lévi-Straussian terms it is like having to learn roughly the extent and nature of a language before we can appreciate that selection from it which is a particular speech. But open systems are not traditionally very satisfying to us (more of Stockhausen's break from this tradition later); all our masterpieces are closed systems in which we feel a total space to have been 'rounded off', all the mooted possibilities to have been treated; we feel that nothing has been omitted and nothing is extraneous. In specific dimensions this is clearly manifested as the tonal system or as the cyclic choice of sets used by Schoenberg (circles of minor thirds in the *Orchestral Variations*, *Fourth Quartet* and *Violin Fantasy*, for instance) and Webern (multiple functions of the last note of the sets linking with the new sets, as in the *Piano Variations*, movements 1 and 2 (2 sets), or the *First Cantata* (4 sets)), or as the larger groups of inter-related sets which, Babbitt says, possess the quality of closure since they are symmetrically related to each other and disjunct from any other possible set or group of sets, and which he used as a total group to define precisely the content and extent of his own works.

In parenthesis, I might mention the view sometimes aired that it would have been much better, and more artistically creative, if all those hackneyed 'favourites' of the concert hall had been written with adjustable section orders and other variables. Each new performance would have been something to look forward to with joy and new expectations! It does not take much perspicuity to see behind this view a distaste for the works to which it is applied; had the works been loved, one would hardly want a hairpin changed. Even Mahler's amazing revisions of Beethoven's 9th,* for instance, spring from the ardent quest for an optimum object, rather than from a desire to create novelty and 'flux'.

* See Mahler's conducting score in Southampton University Library.

Generalisations cannot be made across the two art-concepts.

The other important point about Stockhausen's innovation is that 'the structure of the piece is not represented as a sequence of development in time, but rather as a *directionless time-field*'.† Although the groups themselves must flow forwards, are irreversible, their order is reversible, especially as one's experience of different performances accumulates. This point takes us right into the future of Stockhausen's oeuvre, although it has important historical predecessors in the palindromic nature of both pitch and rhythm in Webern's serial music and in Messiaen's 'non-retrogradable rhythms'.

Before going on to these 'open' forms, however, mention must be made of the important electronic piece *Gesang der Jünglinge*, Nr. 8 (1955–6) which in some senses is quite close to *Gruppen*. In talking of the latter work, I referred several times to electronic music concepts which seemed to be influencing it, though Stockhausen very rightly warns against too easy an equation of two very different sound worlds. 'The structure of a work and its material are one and the same thing,'‡ he says; and if one is envisaging a continuous time scale which stretches from pitch to rhythm then it is no longer so easy to view composing simply as a matter of arranging in time the possible notes playable by the possible instruments. In *Gesang* only the sub-material is unstructured, that is, the sine tones, noise, etc.

† *Die Reihe*, vol. 3, p. 36.

‡ 'Actualia' by Stockhausen, *Die Reihe*, vol. 1, p. 51.

which were the raw material of all pieces made in Cologne studio at the time. From this sub-material and from the sub-material of a recorded boy's voice singing the *Benedicite* in German are constructed three scales, which, needless to say by now, are serialised. They are: 1. the scale between dark and bright timbre; 2. the scale between purely harmonic spectra and random noise bands; 3. the scale between darkest and brightest noise. All these can be varied continuously by electronic means. The same scales are applied to the non-electronic sub-material, the boy. In singing he uses scales between: 1. dark vowels (u) and light vowels (i); 2. vowels and consonants; 3. dark consonants (ch) and light consonants (s).* This is the material.

He also selects and arranges it to make certain formations: 'The selection and composition of material is one indivisible conception. Six scales were selected for the pitch level system. As in earlier works they represent the "interval" relationships between elements, whether they be harmonic or melodic ratios, or those between sound and phones (single speech sounds), sound groups or pitch "regions".'† These 'interval relationships' can be used in any dimension. Stockhausen takes a ratio such as 3 : 2 and applies it to two frequency figures, two measured duration figures, two formant region figures (to change the timbre), two loudness figures by a rather more empirical method based on an intuitive scale of perception (which he explains), and two locations in space – the sound coming from a point intervallically related to the last point around the circle of loudspeakers.

But perhaps the most impressive and original scale used is that between the two camps – voice and electronic sound, human and machine, and related to it – that between discursive meaning and pure sound. At those moments where one realises that a sound one had initially thought of as a vocal one turns out to be an electronic one, and *vice versa*, the unity of the two contrasting elements is apparent, and apparently submitted to a higher ordering that transcends the difference between them. One can then hear the untreated voice without discomfort. The same thing happens when we hear a recognisable word treated as a tone colour. Near the discursive meaning end of the scale there are many degrees of intelligibility ranging from nonsense to half-sense to sense, permutations of the word order and inventions of new words, and new syllables. Because the text is very well known, at least to Germans, it can 'be well integrated in purely musical structural arrangements (especially permutational – serial ones) without affecting the literary form, its message or other aspects'.‡ The new meanings suggested by the new words and syllables (*Schneewind*, *Eisglut*, *Feuerreif* etc.) must be most evocative to a German ear, and the process as a whole is very similar to what certain

* There is an interesting historical antecedent in Wagner's thought. For instance: 'The musical instrument is an echo of the human voice, but so constituted that we can only detect in it the vowel . . .' R. Wagner, *Complete Prose Works*, trans. E. Ellis, 'Opera and Drama', p. 307.

† 'Actualia' by Stockhausen, *Die Reihe*, vol. 1, p. 47.

‡ 'Music and Speech' by Stockhausen, *Die Reihe*, vol. 6, p. 58.

writers of Concrete Poetry such as Augusto and Haroldo de Campos, or Max Bense in Germany have been producing. This restructuring of semantic meaning on the space of the page or in the time of the musical piece is only one manifestation of the enormous twentieth-century structuralist movement which seeks to get behind the conventional one-way progressions to symmetrical closed systems of structure, and perhaps 'to the structure of the mind itself'. The movement is as old as the century: Mallarmé (un coup de dés, 1897) '*Subdivisions Prismatique de L'idée*', Pound (*The Cantos*), Joyce, Cummings, Apollinaire, Beckett (Ping etc.), Mondrian (Boogie Woogie series), Max Bill, Albers, Webern's Sator Arepo square, and its application in his music, Boulez's transformations of Mallarmé, and so on.

Piano Piece XI

The overall structure of *Gesang der Jünglinge* is remarkably like that of *Electronic Study 2*; both final sections combine and develop the ideas stated in the preceding sections. Although the violent contrasts are neatly absorbed into this higher form, it is above all they that give the work its alertness, its youthful, early-morning-visionary quality – a sort of Wordsworthian freshness: '. . . when meadow, grove, and stream,/The earth, and every common sight,/To me did seem/ Apparelled in celestial light . . .'

This work ends what seems to me Stockhausen's richest creative period and one of the most artistic and influential groups of musical works of its time.

9

The Early 'Moment Form' Works

There now occurs a short gap in the flow of compositions, and a corresponding change of direction. The personality changes in some inexplicable way, and the musical thought changes with it. Works become longer, slower, more interested in colour experimentation, 'beauty' for its own sake; less formalistic, less rational. There are no more theoretical, scientific articles in *Die Reihe*; Stockhausen's utterances become increasingly 'artistic' in tone. In short, 'Moment Form' has arrived.

Kontakte was begun, but interrupted by a work not yet conceived in the new ethos, though it does not belong with the 1954–7 group either; if anything, it has closest affinities with the 1951 works for reasons that will become apparent shortly.

Nr. 9 *Zyklus* (1959) or 'Cycle' for a percussionist was written as a set piece for the Kranichstein competition for percussionists. A sequence of sixteen pages is set up in a circle

Ex. 39

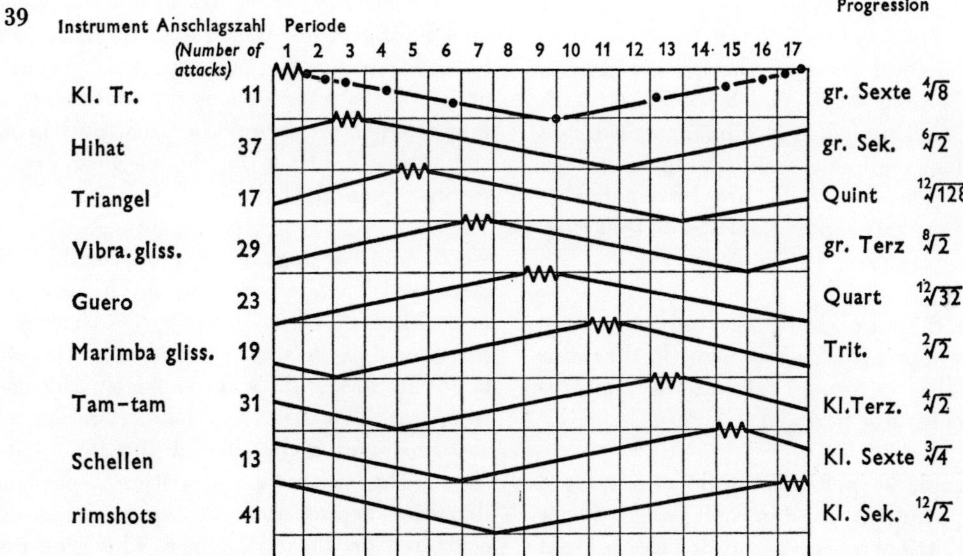

surrounding the player, and he is instructed to pick any starting point and play either way round the complete circle. Thus, it is a sort of open form like *Piano Piece XI*, at least there is no composed beginning and end, but it differs as a circle differs from dots on a page. Even after many hearings one cannot help feeling that it is a simple piece; obviously dimensions are severely limited in a medium of this sort, and the periodic glissandi on the vibraphone and marimba are the crude intrusions of a too-simple tonal world. However, study shows that, typically, it is extremely carefully thought out, and the systematic complexity is considerable.

For an insight into Stockhausen's mind I will try to give some indication of how it was written, using his diagrams.

Stockhausen provided a chart (Ex. 39) to show how nine instruments (left column) play a certain number of attacks (a prime number sequence, next column) over the seventeen periods (one on each of the sixteen pages, except for one page which contains both period 17 and period 1) in a linear ritardando (falling line) or accelerando (rising line) with a certain quasi-intervallic progression (right-hand columns). It can be clearly seen that they reach their climaxes successively.

The next diagram shows the quite separate sequences of principal instruments in the order in which they enter and fall out (each instrument lasts for five periods) (Ex. 40).

And Example 41 (p. 83) shows the number and type of instruments used in each period. There is a symmetrical increase in tone colours from

periods 17 + 1 to period 5, and from period 9 to period 13.

Ex. 40

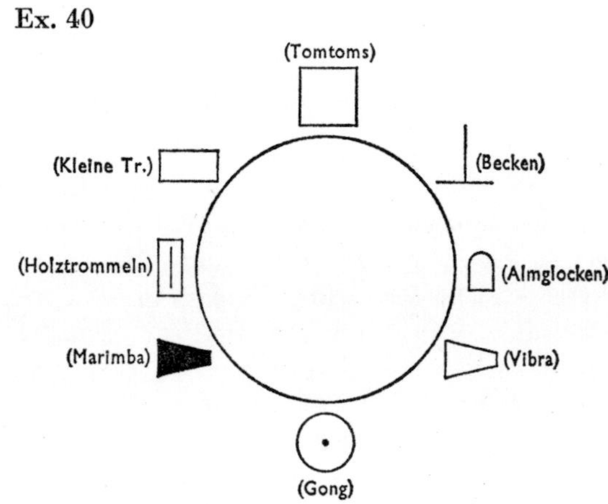

In the periods where many instruments are available and where Stockhausen wants greater indeterminancy, there are various systems of choice, of gestures which may be selected and inserted into the performance. Even the choice of the non-principal instruments is a flexible matter as long as they fulfil broadly the same functions in the plan of dry and resonant sounds.

Each period or page is the same length – thirty measured units whose tempo the performer must himself set. As we progress through the seventeen periods a scale of nine structure-types are used, which move from strictness to freedom. The first type has simple, clear rhythms and well ordered dynamic successions. The ninth has 'statistical' speeds and densities represented by approximate dots scattered on the time-stave. The progression over the whole performance therefore involves a move from strictness to freedom, or vice

Ex. 41

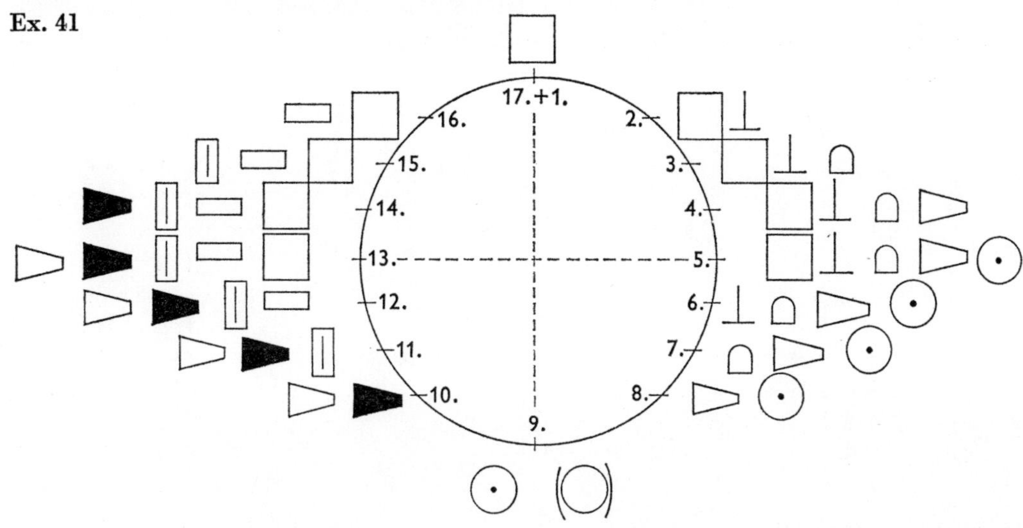

versa if the performer goes the other way around the circle, with an obvious break in theory, but not, as Stockhausen says, in sound between the extremely statistical period 17 and the extremely determined period 1. The following chart shows how the structure-types within the periods, like the instrument types, increase from periods 1 and 9 to periods 5 and 13. The third column shows the number of time units allotted to each structure-type within the period (Ex. 42).

Similarly, the types of sound element (from roll to single stroke) are scaled (1–5), the number of these elements is scaled (a scale with the steep increase of the Fibonacci series – 1, 2, 3, 5, 8), the maximum dynamics of the gestures are scaled (1–5), the dynamic characters (crescendo, all maximum, etc.) are scaled (1–5), and all these scales are serialised and permutated cyclically, their characteristics changing together at the sounds of the *ff* rim-shots of which there are 41 (see Example 39). A further system, a pitch cycle from a large interval (nearly two octaves) to a small one (semitone) determines the widths of the tuned percussion glissandi.

The rigour of *Zyklus* nicely illustrates a point about that distinction between form and content. These forms of Stockhausen described above are clearly audible, but we do not normally think in the way necessary to have them in the foreground of our consciousness. In a Mozart symphony, say, we register the size of the groups of attacks and their regularity or otherwise and the dynamic scales only secondarily to the identity of the musical idea, the sum of them all; and compare it primarily with other *totals* rather than with other *components*. In *Zyklus* the components obstinately refuse to add up to a really cogent identity that we might call a musical idea – the limitation to really very few sound colours

Ex. 42

The whole cycle is divided into two half-cycles. Over the seventeen periods the nine structure-types are distributed thus:

Periods	*Structure-types*	*Durations of each Structure-type*	*Relative Proportions of Structure-types*
1	1	30	
2	2 1	10 + 20	(1 : 2)
3	3 2 1	5 + 15 + 10	(1 : 3 : 2)
4	4 2 3 1	6 + 12 + 9 + 3	(2 : 4 : 3 : 1)
5	5 3 1 4 2	8 + 6 + 2 + 10 + 4	(4 : 3 : 1 : 5 : 2)
6	3 4 2 5	12 + 9 + 3 + 6	(4 : 3 : 1 : 2)
7	4 5 3	15 + 5 + 10	(3 : 1 : 2)
8	5 4	10 + 20	(1 : 2)
9	5	30	
10	6 5	18 + 12	(3 : 2)
11	7 6 5	10 + 5 + 15	(2 : 1 : 3)
12	8 6 5 7	9 + 3 + 6 + 12	(3 : 1 : 2 : 4)
13	9 5 8 6 7	6 + 2 + 10 + 4 + 8	(3 : 1 : 5 : 2 : 4)
14	9 7 8 6	3 + 6 + 12 + 9	(1 : 2 : 4 : 3)
15	8 9 7	5 + 10 + 15	(1 : 2 : 3)
16	9 8	12 + 18	(2 : 3)
17	9	30	

and even fewer pitch arguments are certainly important factors in this – so that we don't have the impression of a *form* organising significant or finely-felt individual ideas, we are left with form alone (as we noted previously to be the case with *Kreuzspiel*). And this lack of tensioned interplay between form and 'content' makes, for me, a dull work.

If *Zyklus* is something of a throwback to the old formalism, Nr. 10 *Carré*, for four spatially-separated orchestras and choirs (1959–60) is certainly a step forward into 'Moment Form'. Moment Form's vital early stages, in which elementary 'material for use' is carefully prepared (viewed as an *area* to be criss-crossed rather than as a *line*), were triggered by the slow time-changes experienced on flights in America. 'A large orchestra of eighty players is divided into four roughly similar orchestras. Furthermore a mixed choir of twelve to sixteen voices is added to each orchestra. For the first performance in Hamburg I chose an almost square hall and had four stages built for the groups.

The Early 'Moment Form' Works

'The four conductors (with their backs to the wall) were: Andrzej Markowski, Michael Gielen, Karlheinz Stockhausen, Mauricio Kagel.

'Voices and instruments are integrated into one sound world. The text is composed according to strictly musical principles: a scale of phonetic sound-differentiations ranges between voiceless consonants and vowels; the text is therefore untranslatable; it is notated in phonetic script.'* And in the programme note for the première: 'This piece tells no story. One can certainly stop listening for a moment if one no longer wishes to or can listen; for each moment is self-sufficient and at the same time is related to all other moments.

'I wish from my heart that this music could give a little inner stillness, breadth and concentration; the consciousness that we could have plenty of time if we take it to ourselves – that it is better to come in to oneself than to stay outside (literally 'go crazy'); for the things that happen need someone to happen to, someone must receive them.'†

Already the reader will be aware of the new tone of voice, the almost mystical obsession with 'feeling' or the 'now'.

In his article '*Momentform*' (1960) Stockhausen voices his impatience with the teleology of musical moments which are always a result of past musical events and an upbeat to future musical events. Why should the poor listener always have to connect the beginning of the piece to the end in one unbroken line? Are not other things more important? Why not have: 'forms of which an instant must not be a little bit of a temporal line, nor a moment a particle of a measured duration, but in which the concentration on the Now – on every Now – makes as it were vertical sections which penetrate across a horizontal portrayal of time to a state of timelessness, which I call Eternity: an Eternity which does not begin at the end of time, but which is attainable in each moment.'‡ (One remembers Rilke's views on music – 'you time, vertical on the direction of vanishing hearts!'.)§

Surprisingly, perhaps, Stockhausen's disdain for exactly measured large scale form dates right back to the *Gruppen* period, though *Gruppen* itself is the ultimate in calculated duration. *Gesang der Jünglinge* was only ended because of the pressure of deadline, so was *Kontakte*; in both cases he had planned and even partially realised further 'moments'. Stockhausen regards them as ended but not concluded in the Beethoven sense, open rather than closed.

Carré, with its four orchestras and choirs, invites comparison with the previous spatial works, *Gruppen* for three orchestras and

* K. Stockhausen, *Texte* (vol. 2), Verlag M. Dumont Schauberg, Köln, 1964, p. 103.
† Stockhausen, *Texte* (vol. 2), op. cit., p. 102.

‡ '*Momentform*' in *Texte zur elektronische und instrumentalen Musik* (vol. I), Verlag M. Dumont Schauberg, Köln, 1964, p. 199.
§ 'Music! Breathing of statues, perhaps', from 'Stanzas for Winter', transl. J. B. Leishman in Rainer Maria Rilke, *Later Poems*; The Hogarth Press, London, 1938.

Gesang der Jünglinge for five loudspeakers. Compared with *Gruppen* the spatial organisation is more sophisticated, or rather, clearer. But in every other way it is a simpler work. Things happen more slowly, at greater length, and only rarely is there a metre; for the most part, time signals are beaten irregularly and approximately according to spatial notation. This has two results: the sound is more inherently beautiful than in *Gruppen* and everything that is notated 'speaks', for it is easier music to play with good tone and there are less problems of getting voices to come through; and secondly, it has much less in it, fewer levels of meaning, less that needs to be remembered to understand the piece as a whole, than in *Gruppen*.

Cornelius Cardew, in two fascinating articles in *The Musical Times*,* has given an account of his role as realiser of the blueprint. All Stockhausen provided initially was the familiar type of plan with pitches, symbols for the rhythmic character, dynamic level, timbral composition etc. of each of 101 moments, a plan which had undoubtedly been plotted as a graph of gradually changing elements, but measured by 'moments' rather than beats or seconds as in more systematic pieces. An element might grow logarithmically over, say, four 'moments'. It was Cardew's job to score out these symbols. He frankly admits that the end result, after all the discussions and cuts, is mostly Stockhausen's (though not without friendly questioning of the point of such a collaboration). But even so, one can see here a significant move towards the improvisatio n of *Aus den Sieben Tagen* (see below p. 113), and away from the precision of *Gruppen*, *Zeitmasze* and *Gesang der Jünglinge*.

Another similarity with *Gruppen*, however, lies in the inclusion of interludes or insertions, or, as Stockhausen came to call them, 'windows' into a further vista. These were only added at a very late stage of *Carré*'s composition, and, as with *Gruppen*, form the most exciting music. There are nine in *Carré*, many of them short and exploiting spatial rotation of sound (Stockhausen was at that time experimenting with a loudspeaker on a rotating table-stand for spatial rotation in the tape of *Kontakte*). For instance, moment 63X throws woodwind chords around, with piano (Orchestra I), vibraphone (Orchestra II), cymbalum (Orchestra III) and harp (Orchestra IV) staccato chords providing another layer. Naturally as the rotation becomes more rapid, the synchronisation must be very precise and exact metrical structures *have* to be used. The effect is astonishing. A music starved almost to death of one of its most important layers of meaning suddenly springs to life and alertness. 69X is another substantial insertion. A soprano D (a ninth above middle C) is rotated one way, and strings and woodwind rotate the other way, five times as fast. 75X sustains the slow, long sounds of the main structure whilst pitting against it simultaneously this other level of metrical music in a way which, again, dramatically raises the music out of its one-dimensionality. 82X is the climax of the added interludes in which frantic directional motion rotates sensationally like wheels of fire, halted with increasing efficiency by suspended motionless chords. This is very reminiscent of the climactic interlude of

* *The Musical Times*, vol. 102, 1961, pp. 619–22, 698–700.

The Early 'Moment Form' Works

Gruppen, groups 118–119. Perhaps your preference for either *Gruppen* or *Carré* indicates what type of musician you are. My experience was to like *Carré* at first (for its beautiful and ecstatic surface), but subsequently *Gruppen* overtook it (for yielding real beauty of a more complex and mysterious sort – despite its occasional miscalculations). But it is a matter of opinion.

The next piece, Nr. 11 *Refrain* for three players (1959) inhabits a quite limited and distinct sound world, though it has affinities with *Carré*, with which it coincides in time, in that it is chordal and in slow unmetrical rhythms. It is for high piano (doubling three wood blocks), celeste (doubling three crotales) and vibraphone (doubling three cow bells and three glockenspiel plates). To this light and resonating sound world are added (as in *Carré*) tongue clicks (five approximate pitches) and short, sharp phonetic syllables – a plosive plus a vowel – which the players have to pitch near the sounds they are simultaneously playing. The effect is like something out of Japanese theatre. Rhythmically the piece is very still, using only approximate durations, and nine times using a notation that requires the player concerned to hold up the performance altogether until his chord has died away.

All this is disturbed by the refrain. The appearance of the score with its semi-circular staves and supplied plastic refrain strip is famous by now; Stockhausen has once again found the exact visual and notational equivalent for the process he has heard in his inner ear. It is possible, however, that as with much avant-garde 'graphical' music the visual conception came first and led to the music only subsequently, but this can only be a guess. The plastic refrain strip, revolving on a central axis in the middle of the music, imposes music on a variable slit of places, compensating for where it arrives in the upper three stave systems by where it arrives in the lower three. It ruffles the smooth surface with a gentle gust of trills, glissandi, clusters, low piano notes and melodic fragments.

There are various other arrangements and compositional rules, but this, like *Piano Piece V*, is decidedly a 'statistical' piece. The pitches are very slow to change for much of the time, but there are certain places where 'change' reaches a statistical high point and a statistical low point. One remembers Stockhausen's comment on Webern: 'a process usually very important for the time-moulding in Webern's music is the fixing of each note in a constant octave-register, and alternation of registers at the most varying speeds; this is one of the most notable means of moulding experiential time . . .'* There are statistical high points for quick change of register, as well as tongue-clicks, phonetic syllables, 'as-fast-as-possible' groups, slow chords etc. The way, for instance, chords will 'fan out' into single notes and vice versa is not arithmetically worked out, but statistical following an overall series of change.

The coda, as in many earlier pieces, *Piano Piece X* for instance, mixes up the elements (including the refrain's) in a sort of 'anti-statistical' way – i.e. there is no statistical predominance of any one element, they are

---

* 'Structure and Experiential Time', *Die Reihe*, vol. 2, p. 72.

finally merged into a complex new unit which one perceives as, if I may descend from the sublime a moment, 'fruit cake' rather than flour, sugar, eggs, butter, almonds, cherries, currants and candied peel.

Whilst Stockhausen was working on *Carré* he was also making experiments in the electronic studio with a rotating loudspeaker which was surrounded by four microphones. As the loudspeaker moved from one microphone to another, so the sound would increase and decrease in each of the microphones in turn, and if recorded on four tracks and played back in a hall with four loudspeakers, one in each corner, the sound could be made to rotate around the hall. These experiments materialised into Nr. 12 *Kontakte* (1960) which can be played as just a tape, or with piano and percussion added. (There is even another version with yet more added to the original tape – *Originale*, a music theatre piece which adds actions and other sounds to the tape, piano and percussion! Superimposing things on existing works is a feature of Stockhausen's late style. It says much about the 'openness' of these works that this is possible; it would certainly be impossible, or inartistic, to do such a thing with any of the pre-1957 works.) In the tape of *Kontakte*, Stockhausen uses various totally new forms of spatial movement – rotation at varied speeds and in both directions; '*Flutklang*' (flood sound) sounds coming from one loudspeaker, then successively from others, which gives the impression of the sound flooding through the hall; alternation continuously between two loudspeakers; looping, where the sound rotates in the form of a loop, i.e. loudspeakers I, III, II, IV: and pointillistic patterns of all sorts.

The other important point about the medium used, is that a piano is juxtaposed to electronic noises. Just as with the ostensibly awkward mixture of a boy's voice and electronic sound in *Gesang der Jünglinge*, so here, a continuous scale between the two different sounds is constructed in order to integrate them. This is where the percussionist comes in. He plays a variety of wood instruments (including marimbaphone), metal instruments (including crotales – high bell-like sounds of definite pitch), and skin instruments. The scale runs

↗ crotales
from piano →marimbaphone } → percussion
↘ tamtam

of *almost* definite pitch, such as African wood drums and tom-toms → 'noise' percussion → tape. In the tape part the sounds were made, after a long period in which Stockhausen analysed the acoustical structures of percussion sounds, by impulse-generator, filter, reverberator and ring modulator. They can be reduced to certain general types. Here they are as drawn in the score with approximate descriptions of how they make 'contact' with instrumental sounds* (Ex. 43).

Thus 'contact' can be made between instrumental and electronic sound, although extremely sensitive performers are required – the piano, especially, can easily be too loud or too soft depending on the level of the electronic sound.

The instrumentalists play almost entirely without metre, fitting their sounds into a cer-

* I am indebted to Edward Cowie, post-graduate student of Southampton University, for putting at my disposal his analysis of the work.

The Early 'Moment Form' Works

Ex. 43

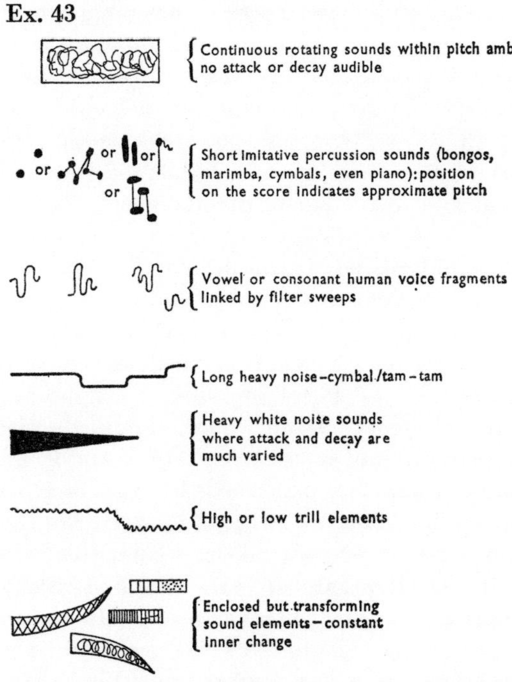

tain space on the page as they think best. Inevitably with a piece which is by no means slow or sparse, as *Carré* and *Refrain* are, the impression of improvisation or rhythmic disorder can be a little disturbing beside the time-structure of the tape which seems both relaxed and precise. But in a performance as sensitive as, for instance, the one Aloys Kontarsky and Christoph Caskel recorded, one's attention becomes transfixed by the beauty of the colour idea, the interplay wherein one is even unsure of distinguishing the piano from the tape, and one moves along the scale from familiar sounds to totally unfamiliar ones with no sensation of losing the meaning.

The variety of timbres and textures is greater than in any previous work, and, again, one must live for the moment alone, for the vivid sense of an *aperçu* – it is not particularly enriching to recall what has gone before or what is yet to come by way of comparison. Though, as so often, an overall behind-the-scenes structural principle is made out of one number, in this case 6. There are six degrees of variation between 'just noticeable' and 'violent' in each of the six dimensions (spatial location, volume, texture, register, speed, instrument family), ordered into six subdivisions within each 'moment'. The six *types* of moment are related by the same range of six degrees of variation, and their specifications delimit the area within which the subdivisions' variations may range, presaging later 'plus-minus' methods.*

The piano and tuned percussion use the set shown in Ex. 44.

Ex. 44

There are no transpositions, but notes jump, and the interval between two notes is frequently filled in, making a cluster; and towards the end of the piece more and more permutations are made. In other words, no over-rigid

* I am indebted to Stanley Haynes for the latter insight.

thought is at work here. It is, broadly speaking, a case of the pitch being suggested by the tape, or else prompted by the imagination to diverge from the tape in some way. In general the instrumentalists help delineate the sections or 'moments'; they change character when the tape does. They also have their spatial role. They are placed at opposite sides of the platform area, and occasionally play a gong and tamtam placed midway between them. At one point the pianist plays his cow bells and then his hihat in a crescendo to *ff* (he has eight percussion instruments to play as well as the piano) and then leaves his seat to play the central tamtam *ff*. At the same time the percussionist plays his cow bells and then moves into the middle to make a crescendo on the gong (while the pianist is still playing the hihat), and at the point of the pianist's *ff* on the tamtam the percussionist makes an *ff* stroke on the gong. At the same time, also, the tape emits loud tamtam-like sounds. Through the world of metallic sounds, 'contact' has been made – and simultaneously demonstrated in space.

Kontakte was Stockhausen's first live *and* electronic piece, and must therefore be regarded as something of a turning point; for most of the works composed since have employed the two media in one form of combination or another.

Originale (1961) was written shortly after *Kontakte* on which it is based. Stockhausen describes it as 'musical theatre'. It consists of eighteen scenes in the form of instructions for the *dramatis personae* carefully placed in time-boxes. Each character's actions, in other words, must take a specified number of

seconds or minutes. These scenes are grouped into seven 'structures' which may be performed successively as 'normal', or simultaneously (up to three at once), or both. For simultaneous performance Stockhausen envisages three small stages: to the right, at the front and to the left of the audience.

The similarities between drama, which moves in time through a total form, and music which does the same, have often been commented upon. It is only logical that Stockhausen, who conceived new types of music by imposing external structures on sound, should do the same with 'music theatre'. The form is no longer ostensibly governed by the flow of feeling, but more by structural patterns of the same sort he uses in music. Again, this is a trait of structuralist art. Robbe-Grillet's books, or his film *L'année dernière à Marienbad* are examples. The line – 'this story is already over – frozen' – occurs many times in the film just as the serial coverage of scales gives a frozen quality to the music; and the perforated layers of time-consciousness are similar to the simultaneities of *Originale*. The *tone* of *Originale* is very different, however. There is much that is surrealistically absurd, shades of Pinter (the commonplace) and Beckett. At one point the actors even speak formant rhythms; one actor has three words equally spaced in four minutes, another five words in that time, another eight, another thirteen (Fibonacci series) and another provides a 'noise' band with totally irregular rhythms. Perhaps Beckett seems nearest of all to it as the dramatist of our time most dominated by musical and serial form in his work, and the surrealism of Mauricio Kagel's theatre pieces may have been influenced by it.

The Early 'Moment Form' Works

The piece is built on *Kontakte*, and with interruptions and recorded replays by the sound technician, it runs from beginning to end, with pianist and percussionist performing many specified actions (like making tea) as well as their parts. There is also an excerpt of seven minutes from a *Carré* recording, the slow-moving final sections from about moment 87 to the end, which would follow quite naturally as an expansion of the slow and profoundly beautiful section of *Kontakte* marked X in the score. *Originale* is Stockhausen's main venture into theatre so far, though by no means the only one into surrealistic theatricality, an element that can be traced especially in works involving human voices, such as *Momente*, Nr. 13.

Momente again exploits the 'feeling' rather than the 'thinking' aspects of music. The *form* is open and adjustable, the *content* richly composed. Stockhausen advises us to lose ourselves in each little paradise of sound as it occurs, not to worry about overall repetitional form.

> 'He who kisses the Joy as it flies
> Lives in Eternity's sunrise.'

was the apt motto in Stockhausen's mind at the time. The 'form' consists simply of a formplan which specifies what sort of thing may happen when, with several alternative choices possible. The main formal distinctions are made in terms of colour-textures, melodic textures and durational or rhythmic textures. The actual 'moments' are named accordingly and juggled in the formplan by the performer, making many creative decisions, but also obeying several rules, putting in insertions from neighbouring moments to pre-echo or echo certain events, and following one set or another of arrows through alternative sequences of events. The complexity of the score arises largely from Stockhausen's determination not to write out *Momente*, but to leave it open, flexible. But it must not be thought that this is improvisatory music. All the orderings and inserts must be fully arranged before the first rehearsal, but not necessarily by the composer.

The forces used to supply the exotic and at times ecstatic 'content' are solo coloratura soprano, four choirs of at least twelve singers each, two electronic organs, brass and percussion including the large 160cms tamtam (which Stockhausen uses in *Mikrophonie I*). This tamtam plays a large part in the K-moments of the work (K = *Klang* or timbre). The colours are *structural*, Stockhausen says. He is here continuing what was done in *Gesang der Jünglinge* and *Carré*, namely integrating vocal sounds and instrumental sounds, pitch and noise, sound and silence. For instance, the choirs not only sing but laugh, shriek, shout, speak, murmur, titter, whisper and exhale voicelessly. They also make noises with fingers, hands, feet, tongues and play little instruments which produce noises or notes. For text, Stockhausen throws together fragments from the 'Song of Solomon', the 'Kala Kasesa Ba'u' from *The Sexual Life of Savages* and Mary Bauermeister's letters to him. The soprano part ranges from singing intelligible texts to voiceless consonants. 'Scales' of this sort are covered as in previous works.

Very similar in construction, though almost the opposite in sound is Nr. 15 *Mikrophonie I* for the enormous tamtam mentioned above and six performers, divided 3 + 3. Both use similar types of formplan with moments freely slotted in, but whereas *Momente* used innumerable instruments this piece uses only one. The formplan again is very simple, consisting of thirty-three boxes representing moments allotted to the two performer groups in alternation (one on either side of the tamtam except where the three signs to show the moment's relationship to its successor: either ≜ (similar), or ǂ (different), or ⫩ (opposite); also either + (supporting) or | (neutral) or — (destroying); also either ↗ (increasing) → (constant) ↘ (decreasing). These are the 'rules' to be followed by the performers in selecting their version. Again, the supplied 'moment' sheets are precisely notated, and each one has a name descriptive of its character. Again, also, there are insertions from other moments which pre-echo or echo events, and various cue arrows which may be chosen which will either bring the next moment in at some point in the middle of the one that's already going on, or at its end. (Even, occasionally, at its beginning.)

The methods of 'exciting' the tamtam are very diverse, and are not so much described in the score as is the nature of the sound to be aimed for. Hugh Davies, who was Stockhausen's personal assistant at the time of *Mikrophonie I*'s first performance, and who operated filters and potentiometers in it, notes in his diary that at one of the last rehearsals: 'Stockhausen's wife finds a few things being used as instruments that have been missing from her kitchen recently!'* The durations, volume and type of sounds are notated precisely. These are performed by the first players in each group of three. The second players hold the microphone near the sound source, or move it away along the surface of the tamtam or else away back from the tamtam. In the first case the sound itself gets softer and the reverberations sound well, in the second case the reverberations get softer and the sound itself sounds well. This part, together with symbols for a cup to collect the sound more or less into the microphone, is carefully notated in time:

Ex. 45

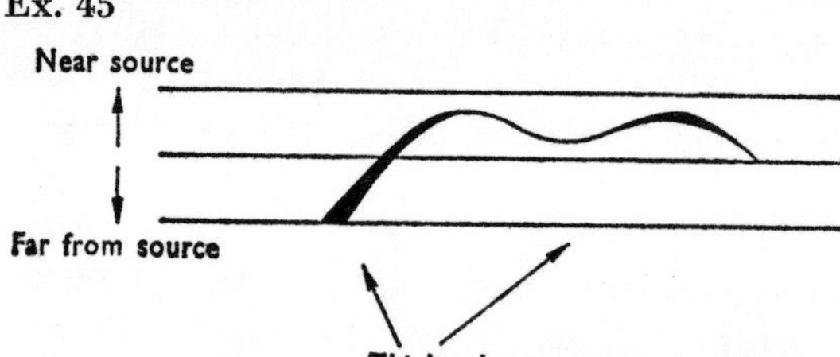

The third performer of each group operates a band pass filter and volume controls, for which he has precise band widths and dynamic levels specified.

The piece is obviously a *tour de force*, something totally new achieved by painstaking trials and errors, once and for all. It can be very long, twenty minutes if the earliest cue arrows are taken, much more if they are not, and it is formally and timbrally very limited. But if one can submerge oneself into this giant mixing machine with all its complex reverberations (actions may reverberate and effect other actions for some time afterwards) it cannot be denied that a totally new experience of sound is offered, as well as an exhaustive knowledge of the complex nature of one simple object – a microcosm of 'moment-form' technique.

* 'Working with Stockhausen', by Hugh Davies, *The Composer*, vol. 27, p. 11.

The Early 'Moment Form' Works

I have left Nr. 14 *Plus Minus* (1963) until now, although it was composed between the beginning of *Momente* and *Mikrophonie I*, because those two works belonged together in type. *Plus Minus* marks an altogether new departure; I shall never forget the incredulity, bewilderment and hostility in the seminar that Stockhausen gave on it at Darmstadt shortly afterwards! Fundamentally, however, it is no different from the formplans of *Gruppen* and *Carré*, the sole novelty lay in publishing it as 'his' work when it has yet to be realised, one's notions of 'the work of art' had to be widened a little, that's all.

It consists of seven pages of 'forms' symbolically notated, which may be realised by up to seven players simultaneously (instruments not specified), and seven pages of notes. One must beware of calling these latter the 'content' which is inserted into the 'form', because by 'content' one means something much more precise and finished – the small scale 'feel' of a phrase or gesture with its dynamic hierarchy of upbeat and stress and registral and rhythmic attributes. The notes provided are simply more 'form' of a different sort, and the realiser must then, according to thirty-five rules, make a great many decisions of his own as to the 'content' he wishes to insert into these forms. They operate, incidentally, on the following set and its inversion:

Ex. 46

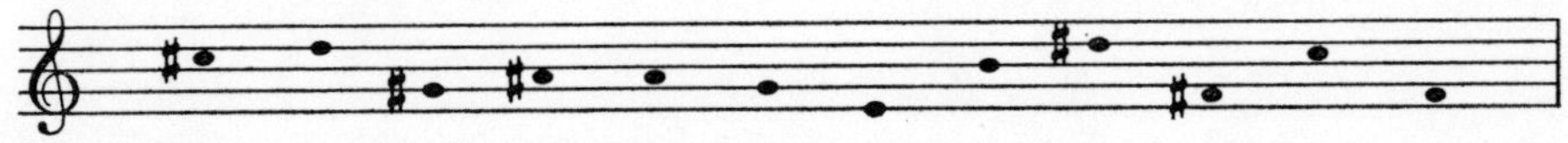

and offer an insight into the different types of set-expression, by *gruppetto* segmentation and jumbling, by band widths of clusters (as in *Gruppen*) following the intervals of the set, by the isolation and development of each interval in turn, etc.

But the linear figurations just described are really secondary to the 'central sound' of each structure, which is also indicated on the notes pages, but as a succession of seven *chords*, each of a different density. One central sound and one linear decoration is specified for each event. To them are added sounds of indeterminate pitch. The seven different *types* of event resulting from different combinations of the above are the basic elements of the piece which are then given instructions on the degree to which they should wax or wane in quantity, in registral height and in volume.* As with the formplans of other works, *Mikrophonie I* for instance, symbols for changes of behaviour are always directly related to what is audible in terms of information theory, to what the listener will perceive as new information or redundant information. In works published at the *Plus Minus* stage, the information theory is the work, and performers must be found who can implement the theory in sound.

* The distribution of *types* over the seven pages is (as with other factors) governed by the Fibonacci series, as Stanley Haynes has pointed out to me; each type occurs either 1, 2, 3, 5, 8, 13 or 21 times on each page.

If I have touched on nearly every work up to 1964, it was to lay out the most crucial aspects of Stockhausen's mind as they moved from one type of form to another, one type of 'content' to another. It seems that nothing written since then changes direction quite so radically, and so the remaining works may be dealt with more informally.

10

The Later 'Moment Form' Works New Achievements in Electronic Music

The only major work I have not touched on prior to 1964 is the revision of *Punkte* for orchestra. The early work, as its title implies, belongs to the highly formalised pointillistic period, and dates from 1952. It serves as a background on to which Stockhausen imposes, ten years later, an elaborate foreground, a text on which he composes a far-reaching variation; each 'point' or single note or notes becoming the centre or pedal point of an elaborate group which surrounds, engulfs, develops or contrasts with it. The result is impressive in the manner of *Gruppen*, there is precise control and much in the detailed texture to extend the experience on repeated hearings. It is a work best understood and analysed as a whole in terms of related group structures, but to do that would be to go well beyond the confines of this book.

Stockhausen has, since 1964, written a fairly constant flow of works. Nr. 16 *Mixtur* for orchestra, sine wave generators and ring modulators (written rather quickly in the summer of 1964) and Nr. 17 *Mikrophonie II* (1965) for choir, Hammond organ and four ring modulators are Stockhausen's first works to exploit the ring modulator. This is a device into which two or more simultaneous notes may be fed (through a microphone), which adds the frequencies together and sounds the resultant note, and also subtracts the frequencies from each other and sounds that note. If one of the frequencies is below 16 c.p.s., as it often is in *Mixtur*, a *rhythmic* transformation of the sounds occurs. The ring modulator's use led to, again, a unique and distinct sound world. 'The "what" (material) is not separable from the "how" (the forming). I would never have composed as I did, had the "what" of this process not had very specific characteristics which lead to a specific "how". For example, when one uses ring modulation, one must compose particular kinds of structures – simple superimpositions, many tones of long duration, not-too-rapidly moving layers – since ring modulators create dense symmetrical spectra from simple material, and this can easily lead to an overweight of noise or a stereotyped colouring of the sounds.'*

Of course, paying respects to the exigencies of sound *per se* rises in a sweep from the bad (?) old days when structures were structures and medieval music could be played sung or whistled on anything to hand, *The Art of Fugue* almost likewise, and even Mozart

---

* Record sleeve note by K. Stockhausen for *Mikrophonie I* and *II* (BS 72647).

could sanction the replacement of oboes, horns and strings by a string quartet (in the three piano concertos offered to a publisher in 1783) or clarinets by violin and viola. Stockhausen stands at the top of this sweeping line of increasing inseparability of sound and form which had grown throughout the nineteenth century. And yet, typically, Stockhausen could see all this and wrote his own 'abstracts' as well – *Plus Minus* for unspecified instruments, *Solo* for unspecified melody instrument, *Spiral* for unspecified instrument or singer, *Poles* for two etc. This implies no contradiction in Stockhausen's personality, only that he likes to concentrate rather exclusively on, and to some extent separate, one aspect of the compositional process in each work. Here it is allowing sounds to grow organically into their own shapes, there information-theory-type thought,there concentration on a sumptuous detail (the 'now'), there a serial trajectory over a whole work, and so on. I've already indicated many instances of how this may be discussed in terms of 'form' and 'content'.

Both *Mixtur* and *Mikrophonie II* consist of fairly lengthy 'moment'-type sections. In the former case each one of the twenty moments has a title indicating its character ('Points', 'Mirror', 'Blocks', 'Dialogue', 'Steps', 'Pizzicato', 'High C', etc.), and the given order in which they are played is variable (reversible, or in a few cases, interchangeable). Four of the five orchestral groups – percussion are separately amplified – that is to say, woodwind, brass, pizzicato (strings and harp) and strings (bowed) are fed into four ring modulators simultaneously with the sounds of four sine wave generators – one for each group – and the result of ring modulating the orchestral group with a specific sine tone is then amplified and put out through loudspeakers. The louder the instrumentalists play, the more the microphones pick up to ring modulate, so unless the volume controller in the centre of the hall turns the loudspeaker output down, it is only the soft sounds and the *very* loud sounds which are easily heard as natural orchestral timbre. Obviously, as in many other works, the scale used is the familiar one bridging the gap between the known and the unknown, the orchestra, and its total distortion in ring modulation, with all the stages in between.

The sine wave generators should never be heard as such, they are simply the factor which makes orchestral sounds alter, or glissando around at various speeds as they interact with the orchestral pitch. Much the same shadowy role is performed without the glissandi, of course, by the Hammond organ in *Mikrophonie II*, though in addition it often supports the singers' pitch – giving in ring modulation a sum tone of an octave higher and a difference tone of zero. The twelve singers are divided into four groups, 'fed' as before, into four ring modulators, amplifiers and loudspeakers. The 'moments', proportionately related, as in some of the other works, by the Fibonacci series, exploit all aspects of the voice, from song to surrealist theatre. Much of the text is drawn from *Einfache Grammatische Meditationen* by Helmut Heissenbüttel which has the advantage of being suggestively meaningful if ultimately meaningless, and good for repetition, permutation and jumbling up generally. It is a study in how far you can twist grammatical structure and still suggest something. A typical line for the sopranos:

The Later 'Moment Form' Works

'like a confused, toothless old crone, enraged: ⟦: "talking intersects talking and there is there is none none":⟧

Mikrophonie II is the first of several works which quotes from Stockhausen's past oeuvre. In *Carré* Stockhausen introduced the idea of 'windows' looking into a further vista, and here that further vista is *Gesang der Jünglinge* (at the beginning), *Carré* (soon afterwards) and *Momente*, in each case the most ecstatic and memorable sections – 82X of *Carré*, for instance. One has the impression of remembering them in a dream, or faintly glimpsing them in the mist, for they are loud passages here reproduced very softly usually over choric whisperings. The tone of 'dream' or 'trance' or what is sometimes (falsely) called 'mysticism' becomes increasingly prevalent in works of this period, reaching something of a culmination in *Aus den sieben Tagen*, itself conceived in a state of meditation.

Having exploited the possibilities of the ring modulator in live performance, Stockhausen goes on to write a work which exploits the possibilities in an electronic tape, *Telemusik*; and further, a work that exploits the possibilities in live performance of another piece of electronic equipment, the time-delay tape loop, or feedback – *Solo*.

Nr. 19 *Solo* for melodic instrument and feedback was written in Tokyo during Stockhausen's visit there in 1966. As the type of instrument is not specified, this work obviously belongs to the category in which symbols or words are provided for the creativity of the performer to 'realise'. It is one of those works in which the composer's emphasis falls on form rather than content – hoping the performer will supply the latter. He does, however, provide six pages of notes with abstract timbral differentiations, fairly conventionally notated, from which the content should be built – all six will be at least partially used in every performance. The hierarchy of sections is set out overleaf.

Choice for the soloist is necessary in the following ways: 1. he must choose a form scheme (one of six sheets); 2. for each of the six 'cycles' of a form scheme he must choose a page of music; 3. he must choose three types of timbre (e.g. mutes) other than his normal tone to comply with instructions in the music; 4. according to symbolic instructions for each cycle he must arrange either (a) the systems of music or (b) the 'parts' of the systems or (c) the 'elements' of the parts in his own order, selecting at random up and down the page. Or these three possibilities may have to be mixed. (This is a vast extension of *Piano Piece XI*.)

Before discussing the form any further, it is necessary to explain the electronic set-up. The soloist plays via a microphone into a tape recorder which records him. The sound travels along a tape loop (adjustable) which gives a delay before being played back over stereo loudspeakers. This same sound on its way to the loudspeakers is in addition diverted back on to the (stereo) recording head, which for some of the time will therefore be recording both the live soloist and his time-delayed recording. This time-delay is always set at the length of the 'period', so a cycle consists of, say, eleven equal periods of six seconds each.

Three assistants are used to 'play' this system. Always following the score, and varying from

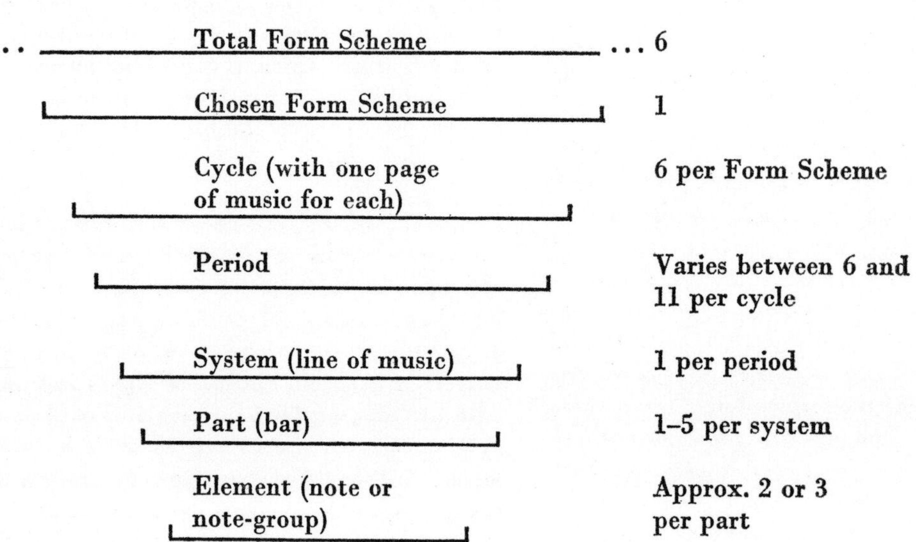

period to period, the first controls which stereo channel the soloist will be recorded on by opening or closing his microphone pick-up potentiometers, the second controls by similar means how much of each channel is fed back to be re-recorded, and the third controls the level of sound issuing from the speakers in a more intuitive way – he should sit near the soloist and 'react' to him; when both channels are open together he should use 'stereophonic alternation (irregular ad lib.) . . . between the speakers at various speeds, sometimes extremely rapid', and create distance effects. In addition the first two assistants are expected to perforate the sound when it's on their equipment with short closings of their potentiometers a specified number of times each period.

The net result of this system is that solo sounds, once performed, may recur at the same time point in the period for as many periods as required, whilst the soloist can go on to play different things over them.

So far, then, we have a selected form from the soloist put into a sort of perforated many-layered canon by the electronic equipment. But there is an interaction between the two as well. The soloist is instructed to play either (a) polyphonically with the feedback or (b) chordally or (c) in 'blocks' (see Ex. 47).

In addition, he does not simply play his arranged page of notes during the cycle concerned, but may be instructed to compare it in a specified way with the next or previous page (to 'anticipate' and to 'remember' things as Stockhausen puts it), or to compare it with the feedback. Here again we get 'information theory' criteria of change: ≈ means 'approximately the same', ≠ means 'different' and ⫲ means contrary.

Ex. 47

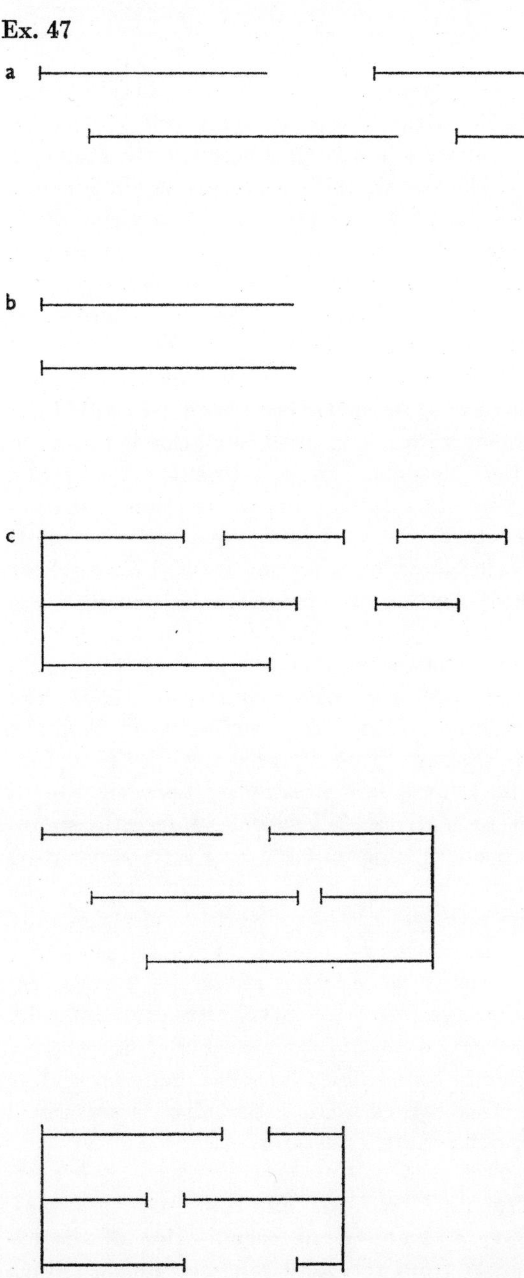

It is evident that the system is the piece. Any precise relationships which existed on the sheets of music are certainly destroyed by their atomisation and rearrangement. The formal structure lies in the difference between the six cycles of any performance. Each has its characteristic ('blocks' etc.). The cross-references of one cycle to another may give a possible small amount of repetition, but they may equally well not. The creativity of the performer in adding together systems and parts and elements is vital, though he has not much leeway to construct any substantial 'ideas' of his own, but in any case, to compose with so many hundreds of thousands of alternatives possible (as opposed to the comparatively few of *Piano Piece XI*) evinces an amazing faith that all precise relationships within the rules will be equally good, or perhaps matter equally little, which latter supposition is lent support by Stockhausen's cavalier addition of parts of *Hymnen* to the DGG gramophone recording of *Solo*! This is excused on the grounds that it will compensate for the loss of the spatial effects – which are indeed very beautiful, perhaps the best aspect of the piece – but at the same time it throws into some doubt our confidence that the composer wishes to hear with precision and sensitivity one note (one group) *vis-à-vis* another in other pieces, where the notation *is* precise.

No such doubts can be sustained in the electronic pieces, however; they are immutable, object-like. And it is to his sixth work in this medium that I shall turn next.

Nr. 20 *Telemusik*, a five channel electronic work, was realised in the amazingly short time of just over five weeks – 23rd January to 2nd

March, 1966 – in the Electronic Studio of the Japanese Radio, Tokyo. Stockhausen dedicated it to the Japanese people in acknowledgement of his admiration for their 'severe struggle' to build the new Japan; perhaps he sees them as an emblem of his own struggle with the traditions of Europe. 'I have learned – especially in this country – that *tradition* does not simply exist, but that it must be created every day.' Stockhausen visited the Noh theatre, the very centre of Japanese tradition, about thirty times, and acknowledges that it had more influence on *Telemusik* than just supplying some of the multifarious recorded music of which the work is composed. He proudly relates how some Japanese, when they heard *Telemusik*, commented that he had re-created Noh-time.

I will quote what the composer wrote about the conception of *Telemusik* because it gives much insight into the man generally, and into his growing concerns about 'embracing the millions'. In this latter notion, and in the visionary quality one is often reminded of Wagner – Wagner's account of how the beginning of *Das Rheingold* (standing for the creation and also the birth of music) was conceived, for instance, or his description of how a *leitmotif* is born in 'On Operatic Poetry and Composition'.* Here is what Stockhausen wrote:

'The first eight or nine days in Tokyo I was unable to sleep. I was happy about it, because thousands of sound-visions, ideas, movements passed through me while I lay awake. After four nights without sleep and four days of working eight or nine hours in the electronic studio without any useful result (I had to assimilate not only the language, the food, the air, the water, the yes-and-no confusion, but also the different equipment), one vision came back more and more openly: it was what I like – a vision of sounds, new technical processes, formal relations, pictures of notation, human relationships etc., etc., all at once and mixed up and confused in a network too complicated to be defined in one process; it would keep me busy for a long time! In all this I wanted to come closer to an old dream – going one definite step further in the direction of writing not 'my' music, but a music of the whole world, of all countries and races. You will hear these mysterious visitors in *Telemusik*, I am certain – from the Amazon, from the Sahara, from Omizutori, Yakushigi, and Kohjasan, from Spanish village festivals, from the Imperial Gagaku, from joyous Bali, from the high mountains of Vietnam, from China, and who knows from where else. They all wanted to be part of *Telemusik*, sometimes simultaneously superimposed and interpenetrating each other. And I had a difficult time making the new and unknown world of electronically produced sounds open to these guests. I wanted them to feel at home, not 'integrated' in an administrative act, but really related by mutual contact of their essence. I don't know exactly how I did it, or what made me go like a moon-struck man, but I believe I succeeded in composing *Telemusik*.'

Telemusik consists of thirty-two sections. Over and above the organisation of the excerpts from folk and religious music (which

* 'On Operatic Poetry and Composition' (1879 Bayreuth Blätter); Richard Wagner Prose Works, vol. VI, trans. W. A. Ellis, 1895, p. 170.

are much less structured than the permutated boy's voice in *Gesang*) and the purely electronic elements stands a superstructure which is fairly symmetrical. Each section is introduced by a clear sound from a Japanese temple instrument. The length of each section is determined by the pitch of the instrument used. The *Keisu*, the principal metal plate chime instrument used in the Buddhist ceremony to demarcate sections in a way similar to that in which the Catholic sanctus bell is used, divides the work into three parts of 10–11–11 sections respectively. In the Buddhist ceremony 'the prayers and holy scriptures are read in a simple chanting style like that used for similar sections in many Christian services. Responsive singing between the cantor and the priests occurs during the section in which the priests rise and make obeisance to their god. It is interesting to note that this ceremony, like the Shinto dances . . . is often repeated in multiples of three.'* The higher bell sound of the *Rin* introduces sections 8, 16 and 24, making a very slow four-against-three formant rhythm with the *Keisu*. The *Mokugyo*, a large deep-toned Chinese temple block used polyrhythmically to great dramatic effect after the *wasan* (final hymn) in masses of the Jodo sect, introduces every sixth section; the *Bokusho* (wood block sound) introduces every fifth section except where this is already introduced by one of the previously mentioned instruments, and the very high *Taku* (wood-block) introduces every second section, with the same provisos applying. Thus this scheme, whatever the difficulties of hearing formant rhythm on this ultra-macrocosmic scale may be, shows another development of Stockhausen's all-purpose theory of time.

The content of these exactly proportioned sections is complicated and often spills over into the succeeding ones. There is a lot of ring modulation of one filtered strand of sacred or folk music with another or with electronic sounds, making for very dense textures in which one can overhear the strains of Radio Seville and Radio Vietnam through the static, suggestive of a sort of global village to which one stands in a relationship partly of radio-wave interconnection, partly of extra-sensory interconnection, and partly of brotherly empathy. But the development of the sacred bells is perhaps the most musically significant element, for they not only strike the musical time-divisions, they also develop through the piece up to section 31, where the high static-obscured filtered music from early sections becomes very high bell sounds with something of the timeless beauty of the end of *Les Noces*, and underneath, four deep and splendidly hieratic temple bells are ring modulated with sine tones and, as in *Mixtur*, made to change pitch while resonating. *Telemusik* is surely the best work of its type. That it ignores more specifically *musical* types of experience is obvious, and, to my mind, amply compensated for by the intensity of artistic vision and the exquisite evocative quality of much of the sound structure. The 'quotations' are treated with the greatest discretion, and the length of the work is appropriate to its material.

Stockhausen's next pieces continue this theme of 'writing not "my" music, but music of the whole world', sounds that may be plucked from the air by radio.

---

* William P. Malm, *Japanese Music*, Charles E. Tuttle Co., Tokyo, 1959, p. 69.

Nr. 22 *Hymnen* (1966–7) is electronic music to which Stockhausen has added schematic, rather than detailed, parts for six of the players with whom he has since this time worked and toured the world. He has also more recently added material, again rather free, for orchestra to two of the sections. The theme of *Hymnen* is the electronic transformation of recorded national anthems, and each of the four sections (called 'regions') so far is dominated by one of them. The banality of the basic material is used as a deliberate springboard for complex transformation – the more memorable the theme, the more it can be twisted in the 'variations'. There are passages of speaking, such as when 'red' is spoken in four different languages from the four loudspeaker groups round the hall. The 'openness' of the work is characteristic: '*Hymnen* for radio, television, opera, ballet, record, concert hall, church, outdoors. . . . The work is so composed that various scripts or libretti for films, operas and ballets may be prepared for it. The ordering of the characteristic parts and the total duration are variable. Depending on the dramatic requirements, regions may be lengthened, added or left out.'* There is a new openness also in Stockhausen's acceptance of the *objet trouvé*; he says that his previous preoccupation with inner worlds of fantasy is here joined through mediation in a higher unity with the concrete external world of everyday sounds and noises† (whose inclusion may perhaps owe a debt to Varèse's *Poème Electronique* of 1958), ending with 'pluralism' and 'monism' grandly united in the 'Utopian realm of *Hymunion in Harmondie unter Pluramon*'.

* Note for DGG record sleeve by Stockhausen, translated Gregory Biss and Rolf Gehlhaar.

† Karl Wörner, *Stockhausen: Life and Work*, Faber, London, 1973.

Hymnen is basically a unification of two worlds, namely pure sound structure and 'found' sound objects with all their associations. They are electronic sounds and concrete sounds respectively. Stockhausen makes the further distinction that they are also the inner imaginative world, and the external perceived world. Their unification is one of the fundamental processes and tasks of life, the forging of links between our deepest image-making selves and the external world, without which that world remains dull and merely utilitarian. Throughout *Hymnen* everyday, 'external' sounds, whose 'meaning', because it is so familiar, strikes one more powerfully than their attributes *qua* form, are modulated by electronic 'imaginative' ideas and thereby lit up as 'form' and at the same time their 'meaning' attributes are transformed. The constant mediation between the two worlds dissolves their difference. Let us see how the forty-odd anthems and sundry other recorded and short wave radio sounds are arranged in this 113-minute work, in many ways the most personal and clear of all his recent output. I should warn the reader that in the rough description that follows, many associative words are used to describe sounds that have been hitherto unnamed, and that it is vital for him not to be seduced into thinking that that is their meaning; he must forge his own links, make his own images – those that will do most for him – and they will almost certainly be different from mine!

Stockhausen describes the first region, which

he dedicated to Boulez, as having two 'centres', the 'Internationale' and the 'Marseillaise'. These anthems are used more than any others. The essential idea of the region, however, is a development of the very first sounds, the sounds of a short wave radio receiver (or several of them) being rapidly switched through the stations. One has the sensation of being swept off one's feet and blown round the world, catching fragments of national anthems, morse code, static and speech (a newsreader saying 'United Nations') as you go. There is a feeling of excitement and human commotion, an extrovert atmosphere which pervades the entire region until near its end, where hints of the inwardness to come are first discovered. Nearly all the sounds of the region can be traced back to this amorphous hotch-potch, the boiling primeval ooze from which the new births will come, as Wilfrid Mellers would say, an idea perhaps extended from the tenth piano piece. The first real opposition to this idea is a succession of two 'dominant' chords:

Ex. 48

each tone separately synthesised from a wave form containing many high partials which is restlessly swept by filters and perforated with amplitude modulations (which control loudness). A background of whistles and shrieks and other sounds of commotion always accompanies this event. It is heralded by a brief, thick upward glissando – a sort of signal for most of the events in this region which itself (typically) is developed: its final and most elaborate version, occurring about two-thirds of the way through, transforms a low fog-horn sort of sound into an upward-rushing clamour of distorted human voices which remains suspended at the top of the texture in the 'hissing' frequency range until it plunges down again into recognisably human sounds at the beginning of the second region.

The 'dominant' chords continue to appear and transform at regular intervals (seven times in all) with anthems, glissandi and station-switching fragmentation in between. They are finally phased out with one of the transformations of which Stockhausen is very fond, where the sound is modulated with a slow frequency giving a jerky, shaken effect, the sonic equivalent of stroboscopic lighting.

The restless gibbering of more or less distinctly heard sounds ceases now for the two-minute interlude on the names of 'red' in four different languages, chanted clearly and simply by the composer, some friends and the croupier on a few liturgical tones, ending with 'international red'. Colour, paint . . . likewise an international 'vibration' language?

The next sections are complex. The dominating elements are distant festive singing with brass band, high pitched 'flood-sounds' (like a chorus of crickets), cut into by the loud glissandi already mentioned and burbling, jerky distortions of anthem material. As the Marseillaise begins to make its presence felt so the overall colour changes and more sounds are introduced, principally motoric buzzing sounds, reverberated flue-pipe sounds not dissimilar to the tingling sounds of *Studie 2*, and glissandoing non-harmonically related clusters.

The final section is an impressive fight between loud brass chords, which become ever softer-edged – Stockhausen slows them down and causes the reverberation on them to sound wavery, loose, as if some monster is plunging ever deeper into the black depths – between this and ever more hesitant, nervous textures in which, again, one seems to be whirling through space and time catching soft echoes of vast choirs, flood-sounds, and any sounds that have appeared previously in the region. It is a brilliant passage of sound-imagination.

A last attempt at the Marseillaise is shattered by a big synthesised column of sound, leaving finally only the cricket-like flood-sounds to carry over into the second region.

There is one element more. Four times, every four minutes, a sinister, filtered casino croupier's voice says a few words, such as 'Faites votre jeu, Messieurs et 'dames, s'il vous plaît.' He is nearly always surrounded on either side by complete silence. He seems to be separate, to belong to some other world running concurrently, but hidden. He appears thrice in the last movement with the same words. Does this ambiguous Joycean figure, perhaps a symbol of another sort of internationalism, have the function here that the Japanese chimes had in *Telemusik*: keeper of the musical time?

The second region begins, like the third and fourth, with continuations of the preceding ideas. One can see from this that the work was not conceived in four discrete movements, and that the flexibility ('regions may be lengthened', etc.) is really present and not a factor that is likely to destroy shape. As in previous works, moods change, elements come and go, and large-scale symmetry is not the most vital consideration. The crickets continue to chirr and to transform back and forth into maracas, hung bamboo clusters and the unknown, but all within a narrow range of timbre. Nine very sharply attacked chord-columns cut in to introduce this region's first anthems, among them, 'God save the Queen', in very perforated, fragmented form. As the cricket-sounds at last begin the descent to become the shouting crowds of people mentioned previously, and as the high frequencies are all drained off, so an important new element is introduced, a synthesised tone or tones in the middle to high frequency range. For recognition purposes, it sounds at times like a painful jet whine, at other times like an electronic organ. It is often varied with different speeds of amplitude modulation. In each of its three extended appearances in this region it transforms, broadly speaking, from the harsh to the soft, and in the third appearance it makes an important formal reference *across* the regions in that it transforms itself into the element I described as 'dominant chords' in the first region, which consisted also of synthesised pitch, and this in turn gets mixed up with the Russian national anthem, the only one Stockhausen synthesised rather than recorded, which, with many variations of wave-form (such as fierce saw-tooth waves) and distortion techniques (such as violent perforating) but also with many simple and quiet triads, dominates the region to the end.

The Later 'Moment Form' Works

But let us return from the history of one event to the history of the region where we left it. Shortly after the crickets were revealed as humans speeded up to cricket-tempo, the humans are speeded up to a point in between human and cricket-tempo which sounds something like a chorus of birds, and a little later a flock of geese and ducks. (Real birds are added to reinforce the transformation.) Nothing could better illustrate Stockhausen's theories about the universe's different vibrational levels being different tempi of the same 'thing' – (see Chapter 11). Although Stockhausen may not be wanting to express the extraordinary empathy with birds that Messiaen exhibits in those late pieces where something of the intensity, the higher body temperature, the quicker movements, the higher frequency range of utterance and hearing, the shorter life-span is understood and transferred into the breathtakingly fast, complex and dense bird choruses, yet there is no doubt that Stockhausen's intellectual and intuitive grasp of the idea, vastly extended into Germanic metaphysics, is profound.

The element descends again, becomes human (talking this time) and is eliminated by means of a further echoing descent and retardation into the murky depths.

The main anthem section – mostly the Federal Republic of Germany's and Austria's – is prefaced by a long soft bass note which slowly sinks by semitone steps and is swept by filter changes giving off different vowel sounds (see my remarks on *Stimmung*) and occasionally joined by memories of past sounds. At first the Marseillaise is recalled as in a deep sleep; low, slow, soft-edged. It is significant and characteristic that the first two chords of the Marseillaise were first heard in the murky elimination of the crowd sounds four-and-a-half minutes previously. There is a short and grandiose section for the Austrian anthem (with a slow outward glissandoing prolongation of the last chord of the second line), followed by much complexity (including a ship-launching scene) and rapid changes of texture. The control of dramatic pace in these long movements is the most obvious manifestation of large-scale formal thinking, and this is the pace-climax of the second region.

There was earlier, in the middle of *Deutschland*, reference to the Nazi *Horst-Wessellied*, then, just as we hear a hint in the 'cricket' sound of an African anthem, there is an abrupt switch to an interlude in an electronic studio. Amidst noises of rewinding and switch-clicks, Stockhausen and another are heard recalling that Otto Tomek said that to include the Nazi song created bad feeling, to which Stockhausen replied that he did not mean to do that, it was only a memory. 'Otto Tomek has said, had said, said . . .' each of these versions is used and this prompts them to the notion that the simultaneous presence of different tenses could be taken further, is another aspect of the multi-time layering in musical structure that *Hymnen* is all about.

After this interlude, the previous texture is taken up exactly, and is continually mixed with the colourful marimbas and drums of African anthems, eventually merging into the concluding synthesised 'organ' sounds already described. It is a structured conclusion, with regular alternation between rapid and disconcerting anthem references and the 'organ' progressions, both elements changing a little at each appearance. This region is dedicated to Henri Pousseur.

The third, dedicated to John Cage, is the shortest, and structurally the easiest to grasp. The first 7¾ minutes are devoted to a continuation of the synthesised meditation on the Russian anthem. It becomes gradually more distorted – the main chords are rapidly filter-swept, panned from channel to channel, ring modulated and amplitude modulated (these are the four principal operations in all the music of this element). When the distortion is at its height the same procedure as in region two is adopted, namely that one chord is sustained and gradually allowed to slide down in both pitch and volume, accompanied by its distortions (filtered ring-modulator fuzz), until, after 3 whole minutes, its extinction can no longer be doubted. At the same time, a morse-code idea has been slowly growing and finally loudens to introduce 'The Star-Spangled Banner', over which it continues to hover for a bit as one of those favourite 'permeable' sound elements which does no harm to the clarity of any other idea Stockhausen likes to put under it.

The Russian anthem had the longest, most exclusive treatment of all the anthems. By contrast and appropriately, the American one is the most wildly inclusive. It is constantly losing its identity in some other anthem, often neatly spliced on by means of a pivot chord common to both. The first region may be thought of as pluralistic, with its many international references, the second, with its prolonged meditation on Germany, has monistic tendencies. The third juxtaposes the two opposites in sharp contrast, and as we shall see, the fourth is an act of homage to 'Pluramon', the marriage of the opposites.

After four minutes of considerable vivacity centred on the U.S.A. there follow four minutes (a frequent 'rhythm' in *Hymnen*) of noise, at first reminiscent of an ocean-going liner's engine, later reducing to a deep coloured-noise rumble. Some of the filtering here is violent and alarming, and the distorted radio sounds are distinctly eerie. A desolate seascape is suggested by soughing coloured noise and brief tern-like calls. Out of the coloured noise we hear Stockhausen himself (presumably) transforming 'from one event to another' with a series of unvoiced consonants starting with 'th', which is indistinguishable from the soughing wind, and finishing with something very close to a whistle. There is a short spoken dialogue between Stockhausen and 'David' in two languages: 'We have to get from America to Spain across the ocean in a few seconds', before we get to the goal of the transformation, namely the whistles which traditionally accompany a Spanish singer and guitarist.

The final, 'Spanish' section is the most hyper-extrovert of all. Just as the outgoing American section followed the inward, questioning Russian one, so the even more extravagant Spanish one follows the even more withdrawn 'seascape'. The emotional contrast is widened. The chief interest in this section lies in the multi-layered treatment of the Spanish anthem, which gets faster and faster (without always rising equivalently in pitch), but some levels get faster than others and form mere permeable texture at the top.* Levels of distinctness and indistinctness interweave with levels of sharply contrasting volume in a kaleidoscope of Spanishry. But things are never as simple as they seem on first hearing. What, for instance, are those two prolonged bell dyads doing near the end? They are followed by a third, much higher, which also has a changing continuation, right until the end of the region. They are prolongations of pitches attacked at great speed – the 'rise time' for notes becomes extremely short when the Spanish anthem is played over at such breakneck speed, it becomes similar to the very sharp rise-time characteristic of bells – so Stockhausen has made an association which arose naturally out of the original idea.

The fourth region has fewer types of sound than any other region, thus completing the direction of the work as a whole in its movement from diversity to unity. The main ones may be described briefly as:

1. the Swiss anthem, which started to appear at the end of the third region, is made clear, then increasingly distorted for about nine minutes. Its final choral triad is prolonged into a breathing-rhythm ostinato of soft-edged immensity, impressively treated within narrow limitations by variations of pitch and rhythm, by the addition of what sounds like a host of angelic sopranos, and so on. This prolongation lasts 11¼ minutes. It finally becomes, after a brief break, the breathing of a solitary sleeping man, apparently lying quite still – an almost disconcerting phenomenon after all the elaborate spatial movement that the other sound elements have been subjected to. His physical location is disturbingly real. For the final 11 minutes of the work he breathes through the dreaming 'R.E.M.' phase into apparently deeper and deeper sleep, and then shows signs of coming to the surface again with his last breath. All this from the Swiss national anthem!
2. deep, cavernous rumbling, a continuation of this idea from the end of the third region. It becomes deeper and gives way after nearly 4 minutes to:
3. a vibrating sound which varies between 'hard' (tapping) and 'soft' (oscillating). This gives way after about 4 minutes to:
4. a red-hot searing siren-sound, with a fierce cutting edge of high partials, made up of parallel lines falling in steady glissandi, a new one fading in imperceptibly at the top as an old one fades out at the bottom, giving that perpetuum mobile sensation of eternal descent (it was first heard briefly at the end of the second region). Punctuations are added by girl's laughter, distant birds and five shouted names which echo as in a labyrinth of subterranean caves. The fifth of these shouts finally, after 8½ minutes, stops the process.
5. a soft duet of near sine-tones derived from the echo of last shout, moving in and out of exact interval ratios; it calms the air for 3 minutes over the last chords of the choral ostinato (sound-type number 1).
6. the casino croupier, who says: 'Messieurs et 'dames, rien ne va plus' at the climax of the

* An example of permeable texture used low down in the frequency range occurs *under* most of this section: a coloured-noise wind-like rumble, a continuation of and link with the previous section. It is sufficiently soft and spongy in character to absorb harder objects without loss of identity to either.

red-hot parallel glissandi (4), and later, after (5): 'Faites votre jeu, Messieurs et 'dames, s'il vous plaît' twice, the second time surrounded by startling silence, bringing the choral ostinato to its end and marking the beginning of the breathing.

7. seven complex columns of sound which cut across the breathing. They are made up from these elements: an initial violent attack followed by a sustained low pedal note of much energy with a high one at a thrice varied interval above it, memories of the synthesised 'dominant' chord element, of several anthems including the anthems of Ghana, Russia + 'Internationale', 'Internationale', Gt. Britain, India (in that order) and of talking events ('a Chinese store'). The pedals, which frame the recapitulated elements – they are sustained before, during and after them – are finally sounded alone and form the last massive sounds we hear; only the sleeper is left who draws a few more breaths.
8. the word 'Pluramon' spoken slowly as if in a sleep by the breather, and soon afterwards repeated faster with gentle awakeness by the same voice – Stockhausen's own – between an exhalation and an inhalation this time, therefore one presumes by some 'other' than the material body of the breather. This symbol of Stockhausen's obsession for bringing together diversity, the pluralism of black and white comprehended in the monism of grey, he calls the ruling principle of the Utopian realm of 'Hymunion in der Harmondie', to which centre the latter part of this region is dedicated.

Hymunion is a Utopia Stockhausen has often talked about recently: 'What I'm trying to do, as far as I'm aware of it, is to produce models that herald the stage after destruction. I'm trying to go beyond collage, heterogeneity and pluralism, and to find unity; to produce music that brings us to the essential ONE. And that is going to be badly needed during the time of shocks and disasters that is going to come.' In Stockhausen's mind the Utopian fantasy is clearly associated with the sadistic fantasy of 'the fantastic catastrophe that will come . . . killing hundreds of millions of the human race'; it is the 'rebirth' that 'can only happen when there is death. A lot of death!'* Elsewhere he has spoken of destruction by fire. This is one of many points at which my personal interpretation of *Hymnen* touches 'The Ring'. The destruction of the old world by fire in *Götterdämmerung* is the sort of image I see in the extremely fierce and almost painfully prolonged climax of element 4, particularly when the sound is momentarily stopped for the croupier to say in his peculiarly enigmatic voice: 'Messieurs et 'dames, rien ne va plus,' after which it burns in again with the utmost violence. There is also the similarity of technique in handling very long time-spans, the broadly conceived dramatic planes, the use of very easily recognisable material which, in a very large free-flowing form is a workable way of achieving coherence, the contrast between extroversion and introversion, the transition from one to the other achieved by chromatically 'sinking' basses (more especially in *Tristan*) or slow glissandi – the Hindu meditative process of sinking into the self that both composers knew about so well – their shared

* Interview with Peter Heyworth, *Music and Musicians*, May 1971, p. 38.

dislike of Hanslick's 'pleasure in beautiful forms' and music as intellectually frozen architecture,* and so on.

Hymnen is a powerful work, one which if you lower your barriers may well hit deep. To go to a performance of it would not strike me as being necessarily like going to a concert, any more than going to a performance of *Die Schöne Müllerin* would strike me as being like going to a poetry reading. It is a work of 'drama–music' in which the medium is sound and the relationships work in the same sort of musical way that dramatic relationships are musical – characters develop, have progressions one way or another and interweave, over-all pace is carefully controlled, and elaborated by more subsidiary paces within itself. These characters are rather single-dimensional, and there lies my distinction, for the characters I would expect to perceive at a concert would be multi-dimensional, namely highly developed musical ideas drawing on some 'system of reference', tonal, serial or otherwise. The idea of this piece is to achieve richness by superimposing several changing characters on top of each other, or referring to them at wide intervals of time, also by imaginative changes of form and the cross-breeding of two or more ideas together, and also by creating strongly associative moods – more literally 'dramatic' than would be possible in a piece concerned with multi-dimensional musical relationships. It is one of the supreme artistic conceptions of our time, yet one for whose full understanding no musical training whatsoever is necessary.

---

* Richard Wagner's Prose Works, trans. W. A. Ellis, 1893, vol. V, 'Beethoven', p. 77.

Nr. 21 *Adieu* for wind quintet and Nr. 23 *Prozession* are both works in which a lot of freedom is given to the performers. *Prozession* (process on its way) was written for Stockhausen's group to play on tours, and it presupposes a tremendous *rapport* and intelligence from the players, as the players' parts use only +, — and = signs for 'form' and previous works of Stockhausen (again) for material to be shaped into 'content'. The tamtam uses events from *Mikrophonie I*, the fifty-five-chord (an electronic instrument) or the amplified viola events from *Gesang der Jünglinge* and *Kontakte* and *Momente*, the electronium events from *Telemusik* and *Solo*, and the piano uses events from *Piano Pieces I–XI* and *Kontakte*. Performed by Stockhausen's close associates, with his own music as a basis, the result is inevitably pure Stockhausen. In any improvisatory case, failing any other suggestions, any group, confronted with minimal material with Stockhausen's name on the cover will do the same, though Stockhausen has felt it necessary to suggest that groups should listen to his recordings of the 'improvised' pieces as a guide, thus, it seems, defeating the object of allowing the sounds to suggest themselves. Any good performer must have the 'feel' of a piece to play it well. This 'feel' may manifest itself as a visual thing – for instance, as when Ronald Lumsden, in his performances of *Piano Piece V*, sees a little man about an inch in height inside the piano, dwarfed by giant hammers crashing all around him; he says that only when he arrives at some such strong feeling which can unify all his thoughts about a piece is he happy that he can play it well, or indeed that it's good music. And pluses and minuses or a few instructions do not in themselves add up to any such picture. Stockhausen has recognised this danger and has announced his intention of supplying more precisely determined music ('my music') to set the collective ball rolling again.

Adieu for the conventional wind quintet uses improvisation in a more limited sense. In each of the thirty-four groups whose lengths are proportioned, again, in the Fibonacci series (1, 2, 3, 5, 8, 13, 21, 34, 55, 89 or 144 units), the player is given a pitch or pitches and told to play polyphonically with his colleagues, synchronously, in groups of instruments, with constant or accelerating or slowing down intervals of entry, irregularly with small glissandi around the notated pitches, adding free grace notes etc., etc. The full title of the work is *Adieu* for Wolfgang Sebastian Meyer. Meyer was an exceptionally gifted organist, the son of the Cologne oboist who played many times in *Zeitmasze*; he was killed in a car accident at the age of twenty-seven. Stockhausen uses traditional language in a rather eerie way to symbolise the meaning of this event. Four very soft quasi-baroque cadences are interrupted before resolution by the entry of the chord on which improvisation is performed. They define the four 144-unit-long sections into which *Adieu* is divided. At the very beginning, for instance:

Ex. 49

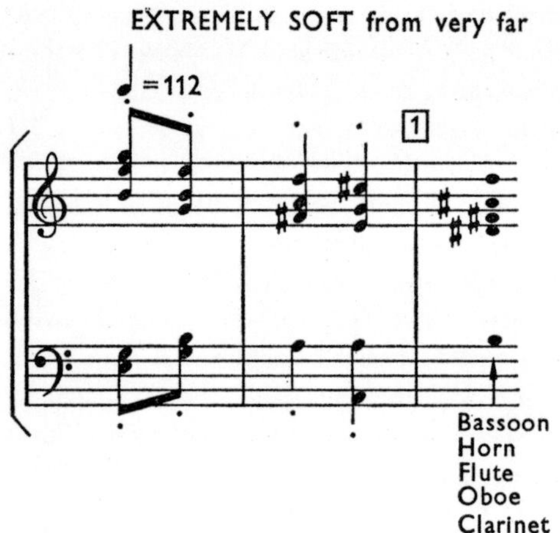

89 units, each unit is MM=40–60

INDIVIDUALLY
VERY LONG DURATIONS
IRREGULAR (i.e. avoid regular rhythms)
GLISSANDI very slow irregular
(small variations around the given pitch)

Nr. 24 *Stimmung* (translated by Stockhausen as 'Tuning' but which can also mean 'mood', 'frame of mind' or even 'voicing') for six vocalists likewise uses very static slow-moving sounds with different ways of repeating the long notes. Also it uses tonal material, but from the opposite end – the novelty consists not in its combination with 'modern music', but in the fact that no composer before (with the exception of La Monte Young and a few other Americans) had considered using only one harmony for seventy-five minutes. Doubtless Monteverdi had thought of it, but had too many adventures into harmonic diversity tempting him to have any time or inclination left for it. Now, three and a half centuries later, those adventures are no longer so tempting. It is a piece based on the harmonic series. The lower harmonics (except the fundamental) are sung by the voices as main pitches,

Ex. 50

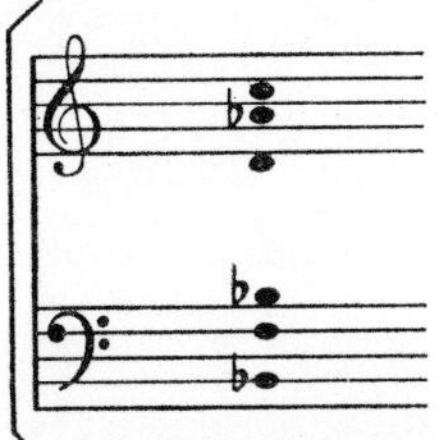

(the chordal texture being relieved by five unison texture sections) but they must train themselves to produce exactly certain spectra on their main pitches, scored in their parts as vowel sounds. Stockhausen always justifies his long static passages by saying that they give us time to go inside the notes and perceive their wave structure and harmonic series content: from *Kontakte* on he would have us re-educate our ears to distinguish the partials of a note, and not be content merely to hear them as a conglomeration, a timbre. There is even an unfinished orchestral work dating from 1960 – *Monophonie* – which uses middle E-flat throughout for constant transformation. Obviously an important precursor of *Stimmung*. It is quite easy to hear for yourself the entries of successively higher harmonics in the vocal harmonic series if you sing on one note a sequence of vowels from darkest to brightest in one 'filter-sweep'. These soft, vibrato-less held notes are constantly changing colour in a notated rhythm – called a 'period' which is repeated over and over again during each of the fifty-one sections – and yet this essentially gentle sound is gently disturbed (as in *Refrain*) by the utterance of a Magic Name, which should be integrated with the rhythms and lip and mouth positions of the singer singing the vowels; and other Magic Names are then offered by other singers who attempt to perform a similar integration until identity has been achieved, and the disturbing ripples absorbed into the calm. Indeed, the whole principle by which the piece moves from one section to the next is that, although a pitch and a vowel-rhythm scheme may change completely, other voices only change gradually until they reach the new identity; and when two little poems by Stockhausen are spoken, odd syllables are to be taken up and 'absorbed' by the other voices. The Magic Names are the names of Gods and Goddesses (each singer has several from one region). The vowel-schemes include odd words, often of sacred or erotic significance – 'hallelujah', 'yoni' – and two short poems which are somewhat surrealist in tone and erotic in subject. They should be spoken 'with a great deal of variation in pitch, without exaggeration, peacefully, gay, with gestures towards the other singers'. To describe the combination of metaphysics, eroticism and playfulness, and the trance-like inaction of this extraordinary and original piece as 'oriental' is a little too easy. In fact it is the westerner's conception of orientialism, such as is commonly found on the west coast of America where the piece was written. It dates, curiously enough, from the very place (San Francisco) and year (1967) of the first Human Be-in when 20,000 hippies demonstrated their brotherhood and the Summer of Love was publicised all over the world, Haight-Ashbury being 'the vibrant epicentre of the hippie movement' as *Time* magazine had it. Most genuine oriental music, however, far from being long, slow and contemplative, possesses quite extraordinary rhythmic vitality.

Nr. 25 *Kurzwellen* for tamtam, viola, electronium, piano, filters and volume controls and four radios again suggests images of America – Cage was to my knowledge the first composer consistently to use radios in music, albeit for rather different aesthetic reasons, (Stockhausen uses radios only to *transform* them); again there is the 'global village' theme of the electronic connection of all men in brotherhood, the theme of vibrations in the air around us 'plugging in to the universe', perceiving the hidden connecting-flow (spoken of by so many mystics and more recently LSD experimentalists), and so on. Here Stockhausen comes still nearer to Cage's 'acceptance of the given sound' (as opposed to enforcing what one's ego likes). He found the work gave '*lasting* metapersonal inspiration, expanses of calm, dimensional plurality, freedom, spaciousness, and of a *medial self-renunciation* transcending all our previous experiences'.* As with *Prozession*, the players are simply given +, — or = signs with a few others pertaining to types of synchronisation with other players. The material, which in the former case was from Stockhausen's own earlier works, is here whatever the radio comes up with on a short wavelength, subject to a certain degree of selection – the player sometimes softly searches for the sort of sound he requires – and always to a certain degree of distortion. As with the bipolarity of *Gesang der Jünglinge* (voice/electronic sound) and *Kontakte* (piano/electronic sound) so here the piece is based on a scale ranging from almost exact imitation of radio sounds by the live performers to their natural dissimilarity. From black to white, as Stockhausen is fond of saying, with all the shades of grey in between.

Stockhausen made a celebratory disc for Beethoven's tercentenary year by using Beethoven recordings instead of short wave events. He made up four Beethoven tapes for the players, proceeding in roughly chronological order, with various obscurations and distortions, and produced what can only be called an unmitigated disaster. *Stockhoven-Beethausen Opus 1970*, as it is called, does not transform the past as Messiaen, back in 1952, showed Stockhausen how to do it, or anything like it. Nor does he descend into the backgrounds and *Urlinien* of Beethoven's structures and rebuild the material from there; he takes scraps of Beethoven as mere local sound (his least interesting aspect) as it appears on some recording or other. Any remnant of Stockhausen's personality is swamped by Beethoven, who in turn is swamped by the irritating distortions. No *tertium quid* emerges; the work is characterless – it has no 'feel'.

* Karl Wörner, *Stockhausen: Life and Work*, Faber, 1973, pp. 75-6.

11

Aus den sieben Tagen – 'Intuitive' Music

Nr. 26 *Aus den sieben Tagen – compositions May 1968* would seem to be a fitting work with which to conclude this study, as it is really the *ne plus ultra* of the works on either side of it and the philosophical kernel of a whole spate of 'ideas for improvisation' which has followed. During seven days in early May 1968 Stockhausen shut himself up, ate nothing, meditated much. The result was a book of fifteen brief sets of instructions, couched, this time, not in practical language, but in suggestive evocative language which has distilled what he wants performers to do to such an extent that what he offers is almost meaningless, it is everything and nothing, an incommunicable essence, the '*unvorstellbar*' of Moses's vision in Schoenberg's opera. Here are some of them translated:*

for ensemble

VERBINDUNG – Connection

play a vibration in the rhythm of your body
play a vibration in the rhythm of your heart
play a vibration in the rhythm of your breathing
play a vibration in the rhythm of your thinking
play a vibration in the rhythm of your intuition
play a vibration in the rhythm of your enlightenment
play a vibration in the rhythm of the universe

mix these vibrations freely

leave enough silence between them

May 8, 1968

for ensemble

AUFWÄRTS – Upwards

play a vibration in the rhythm of your smallest particles

play a vibration in the rhythm of the universe

play all the rhythms that you can
distinguish today between
the rhythm of your smallest particles
and the rhythm of the universe
one after the other
and each one for so long
until the air carries it on

May 8, 1968

* Translated by Rolf Gehlhaar, John McGuire and Hugh Davies.

for ensemble

ABWÄRTS – Downwards

play a vibration in the rhythm of your limbs
play a vibration in the rhythm of your cells
play a vibration in the rhythm of your molecules
play a vibration in the rhythm of your atoms
play a vibration in the rhythm of your smallest particles
which your inner ear can reach

change slowly from one rhythm to another
until you become freer
and can interchange them at will

May 8, 1968

for ensemble

INTENSITÄT – Intensity

play single sounds
with such dedication
until you feel the warmth
that radiates from you

play on and sustain it
as long as you can

May 9, 1968

for ensemble

TREFFPUNKT – Meeting Point

everyone plays the same tone

lead the tone wherever your thoughts
lead you
do not leave it, stay with it
always return
to the same place

May 8, 1968

for ensemble

NACHTMUSIK – Night Music

play a vibration in the rhythm of the universe
play a vibration in the rhythm of dreaming

play a vibration in the rhythm of dreaming
and slowly transform it
into the rhythm of the universe

repeat this as often as you can

May 8, 1968

for ensemble

SETZ DIE SEGEL ZUR SONNE – Set Sail for the Sun

play a tone for so long
until you hear its individual vibrations

hold the tone
and listen to the tones of the others
– to all of them together, not to individual ones –
and slowly move your tone
until you arrive at complete harmony
and the whole sound turns to gold
to pure, gently shimmering fire

May 9, 1968

Aus den sieben Tagen

for ensemble
at first for 3
then for 4, 5, 6, 7 players, singers

KOMMUNION – Communion

play or sing a vibration in the rhythm of the limbs
of one of your fellow players

play or sing a vibration in the rhythm of the limbs
of another of your fellow players

play or sing a vibration in the rhythm of the cells
of one of your fellow players
. . . of another . . .

play or sing a vibration in the rhythm of the molecules
of one of your fellow players
. . . of another . . .

play or sing a vibration in the rhythm of the atoms
of one of your fellow players
. . . of another . . .

play or sing a vibration in the rhythm of the smallest
particles that you can reach
of one of your fellow players
. . . of another . . .

try again and again
don't give up

May 9, 1968

for ensemble

ES – It

think NOTHING
wait until it is absolutely still within you
when you have attained this
begin to play

as soon as you start to think, stop
and try to reattain
the state of NON-THINKING
then continue playing

May 10, 1968

to the player

LITANEI – Litany

For many years I have said it innumerable times
and sometimes written it: that
I do not make MY music, but
only relay the vibrations I receive;
that I function like a translator,
that I am a radio. When I composed in the right way,
in the right state of mind,
my SELF no longer existed.

Now I am trying to reach the next stage,
to connect you, the player,
to the currents that flow through me,
to which I am connected.
I am not trying to make a composer of you in the old sense,
but rather to gain a completely new confidence in your abilities:
so that through me you will be connected
to the inexhaustible source

that pours out through us in the form of
musical vibrations.

Do not try to grasp it with your mind,
you will only disturb it all and make it
impossible.
You must gain the confidence that you will
be able to do it.
I have had it from the beginning.
It is only because of this that I am a short
step ahead of you.
But you must gain it too, otherwise everything that I have received
and want to transmit through you
will be false and distorted.

You may have neither the time nor the
patience
to concentrate consistently and increasingly
better
on allowing whatever must go through us
to sound as undistorted as possible.
That is why I am doing it for you
as long as you cannot do it for yourself.
I will tune you in like a receiver,
but whether or not you sound clear, depends
upon you.

My last experience was KURZWELLEN;
I came as close as I could to you
and to what there is of music in the air.
Now comes the difficult leap:
no longer to transmit man-made signals,
music, tintinnabulation,
but rather vibrations which come
from a higher sphere, directly effective;
not higher above us, outside of us,
but higher IN US AND OUTSIDE.

May 10, 1968

Chapter Eleven

for any number of musicians

ANKUNFT – Arrival

Give up everything, we were on the wrong
track.
Begin with yourself:
you are a musician.
You can transform all the vibrations of the
world into sounds.
If you firmly believe this and from now on
never doubt it,
begin with the simplest exercises.

Become quite still, until you no longer
think, want, feel anything
Sense your soul, a little below your chest.
Let its radiance slowly permeate your whole
body
both upwards and downwards at the same
time.
Open your head on top in the center, a
little towards the back,
and let the current that hovers above you
there, like a dense sphere
enter into you.
Let the current slowly fill you from head to
foot
and continue flowing.

Quietly take your instrument and play, at
first single sounds.
Let the current flow through the whole
instrument.
Whatever you want to play, even written
music of any sort, begin only
when you have done what I have recommended.

You will then experience everything on your
own.

Aus den sieben Tagen

Before you play, you may let your thoughts
run free, you may train the muscles
of your fingers, of your larynx, etc.
But now you know what you think and
train for,
and even the thinking and training
will be completely new, completely different
from before.
Nothing is as it used to be.

As long as you retain this consciousness,
everything you will do will be right and good.

May 11, 1968

There is also a theatre piece, *Oben und unten*, in which a disagreeable and bestial man and two instruments rich in 'noise', such as viola with contact microphone and filter and tam-tam with microphone and filter, provide one strand and a refined and angelic woman with two 'clear' instruments like piano and electronium provide another. A child in the middle echoes words he hears. After delivering their words straight into the audience for at least forty minutes the man and woman dance together and continue intermittently their duet of monologues. No text is given.

These 'compositions' express in essence much of what we have already seen in Stockhausen's previous work. *Kommunion** expresses the brotherhood theme of, say, *Telemusik*; *Verbindung* the theory of '. . . how time passes . . .' *Abwärts* and *Es* the introspection theme of, say, *Stimmung*; *Aufwärts* the theme of a 'serial' scale between two extremes, as in all the middle period works, *Treffpunkt* the 'information theory' theme – the necessity for 'redundancy' in the articulation of 'experiential time'; *Nachtmusik* the theme of 'dreaming' as expressed in works like *Mikrophonie II* with its distant dreamings of earlier works, or the somnolent breathing rhythms at the end of *Hymnen*; and the two longer statements express the relationship to *Kurzwellen* and the musician-as-medium theme generally.

Of course, all of them may be seen as a physical or metaphysical extension of the theory of temporal vibrations as expressed in '. . . how time passes . . .' which Stockhausen sees as extending from timbre through high pitch through rhythm to tempo and large scale form. Indeed he has elsewhere fascinatingly pictured the effect of music itself on man as a stimulus on a vibrating object (to be 'moved' or 'stirred' = to be vibrated), correlating 'being on the same wavelength', 'responding to' with 'vibrating sympathetically' – resonating for longer or shorter periods after the sound itself has finished. This unity of musical time he now extends to the unity of matter, which likewise exists in the form of vibrations in time.

Despite all the associations with modern science (acoustical research, radio communications etc.) these ideas are essentially traditional, extending back to ancient Persian and Egyptian mythological notions about the creation of the world from a single divine resonance. Pythagoras's teaching, in so far as

* There are fascinating connections now being hypothesised between telepathy and quantum physics by utterly 'respectable' scientists. With regard to 'play or sing a vibration in the rhythm of the smallest particles that you can reach of one of your fellow players' see the discussion of the physicist Adrian Dobbs's work in Arthur Koestler's *The Roots of Coincidence*, Hutchinson, 1972, pp. 69–81.

it has come down to us through Porphyry and Iamblichus, contains some of the earliest expressions of them, and they had a great artistic ferment in the nineteenth century and turn-of-the-century theosophy where they border on occultist numerology, as, for instance, in Edouard Schuré's book, *Pythagoras and the Delphic Mysteries** – 'Pythagoras called his disciples mathematicians, because his higher teaching began by the doctrine of numbers. These sacred mathematics, however, or science of principles, were both more transcendent and more living than profane mathematics, which alone are known to our savants and philosophers. In them Number was not regarded as an abstract quantity but as the intrinsic and active virtue of the supreme One, of God the source of universal harmony. The science of *numbers* was that of the living forces, of the *divine faculties* in action in the universe and in man, in the macrocosm and in the microcosm.'

Although Plotinus and the Neo-Platonists and what Kathleen Raine in *Blake and Tradition*† describes as *the* great tradition of European art do touch on the sort of things Stockhausen is putting forward, they are not concerned with them centrally. There is an important difference. The purest neo-platonic thought is never disconnected from the moral aspect. Or, as the purest and greatest successor in the Gnostic tradition, Rudolf Steiner, has said, every step forward in the spirit world must be accompanied by three in the moral world, otherwise you lose the power to tell illusion from reality. The stripping of the ego, advocated, indeed, by all major religions, which will lead to a new perception of the nature of things, means essentially unselfishness and freedom from 'the whirlpool of desire'. But there can be no doubt that Stockhausen has directed strong attention to the existence of spiritual organs of perception present in a germinal condition in all men. They require only to be developed; and the time for this sort of evolutionary step has arguably arrived.

The influences forming Stockhausen's mysticism must date back to his youthful return to Catholicism, and his travel experiences broadened the aspects, and names, of God. The yogic books of the Indian, Sri Aurobindo, were his most vaunted influence at one time (in about 1968), but perhaps it would be of interest to point out the less obvious affinities of Stockhausen with a strong German tradition, of which he continually reminds one. It runs through Meister Eckhart‡ (a favourite of John Cage's also) and later Jakob Boehme, to Schopenhauer and some of the romantic poets and beyond. Novalis (1772–1801) wrote at the beginning of his unfinished novel *Der Lehrling*:

* Edouard Schuré, *Pythagoras and the Delphic Mysteries*, Wm. Rider & Son, London, 1910, p. 84.
† Princeton University Press, 1968.

‡ The similarity between Meister Eckhart, other fourteenth-century German mystics and those that follow them on the one hand, and Upanishadic and Vedāntic monism on the other hand has often been noted (e.g. R. C. Zaehner, *Mysticism Sacred and Profane*, Oxford University Press, London, 1961, p. 181), and it is interesting that this German–Indian axis should be echoed in our day. Sympathy with the overt monism of the Vedānta and Upanishads (in which Sri Aurobindo is so steeped) has not been all that common in European history outside Germany.

Aus den sieben Tagen

'Manifold paths are trodden by men. He who traces and compares them will see strange figures emerging; figures that seem to belong to that great cipher-writing which one catches sight of everywhere – on wings, egg-shells, in clouds, in the snow, in crystals and stone formations, on freezing waters, on the inside and outside of mountain ranges, of plants, animals, men, in the heavenly lights, on sheets of tar and glass which have been touched and rubbed, in iron-filings around the magnet, and in curious conjunctures of chance. In them one intuits the key to this wondrous writing, its grammar; but this intuition will not let itself be pieced together into any fixed forms, and seems to resist transformation into a higher key. An alcahest* seems to have been poured out over the senses of men. Only momentarily do their wishes, their thoughts seem to solidify. This gives rise to their intuitions, but after a short period, everything is again, as before, swimming before their gaze.

'From afar I heard it said: "The incomprehensibility is the result only of a lack of understanding this; (the language) seeks what it already has and what could therefore never be the object of a further discovery. One does not understand the language, because the language does not, and does not wish to, understand itself; true Sanscrit† would speak in order to speak, because speaking is its joy and its essence."

'Not long after this someone spoke: "Holy writ is not in need of any explanation. Whoever speaks truthfully is filled with eternal life, and his writing seems to us to bear a wonderful relationship to genuine mysteries, for it is a chord from the symphony of the universe." '‡

Or, in an aphorism from *Fragmente*: 'Seasons, times of day, lives and destinies, are all, strikingly enough, thoroughly rhythmical, metrical, according to a beat. In all trades and arts, in all machines, in organic bodies, in our daily functions, everywhere: rhythm, metre, beat, melody. Anything we do with a certain skill, we do rhythmically without being aware of it. Rhythm is found everywhere. All mechanisms are metrical, rhythmical. There must be more to this. Could it be simply the influence of laziness?'§

A more recent member of this tradition, and perhaps a direct influence, is Rilke, a poet well known to every educated German. In a famous letter of 1925 to his Polish translator, he wrote: 'We, local and ephemeral as we are, are not for one moment contented in the world of time nor confined within it; we keep on crossing over and over to our predecessors, to our descent, and to those who apparently come after us. In that greatest "open" world all *are*, one cannot say "contemporary", for it is the very discontinuance of time that makes them all *be*. Transitoriness is everywhere plunging into a deep being. And therefore all the forms of the here and now are not merely to be used in a time-limited way, but, so far as we can, instated into those superior significances in which we share. *Not, however, in the Christian*

* Alcahest = a universal solvent of the alchemists.

† Sanscrit regarded by Romantics as the primordial language (Ursprache).

‡ Novalis, *Schriften*, Stuttgart, 1960, p. 79.

§ Novalis, *Hymns to the Night and other selected writings*, the Liberal Arts Press Inc., Library of Congress Catalog Card No. 60–9556, 1960, p. 71.

sense (from which I more and more passionately withdraw), but, in a purely mundane, deeply mundane, blissfully mundane consciousness, to instate what is *here* seen and touched into the wider, into the widest orbit – that is what is required. Not into a Beyond, whose shadow darkens the earth, but into a whole, into *the whole.* Nature, the things we move about among and use, are provisional and perishable; but so long as we are here, they are *our* possession and our friendship; sharers of our trouble and gladness, just as they have been the confidants of our ancestors. Therefore, not only must all that is here not be corrupted or degraded, but, just because of that very provisionality they share with us, all these appearances and things ought to be comprehended by us in a most fervent understanding, and transformed. Transformed? Yes, for our task is to stamp this provisional, perishing earth into ourselves so deeply, so painfully and passionately, that its being may rise again, "invisibly", in us. *We are the bees of the invisible. Nous butinons éperdument le miel du visible, pour l'accumuler dans la grande ruche d'or de l'Invisible.* The "Elegies" show us at this work, this work of the continual conversion of the beloved visible and tangible into the invisible vibration and agitation of our own nature, which introduces new vibration-numbers into the vibration-spheres of the universe. (For, since the various materials in the cosmos are only the results of different rates of vibration, we are preparing in this way, not only intensities of a spiritual kind, but – who knows? – new substances, metals, nebulae and stars.)'*

* Rainer Maria Rilke, *Sonnets to Orpheus*, Hogarth Press, London, 1936, pp. 19–20.

The 'conversion' of the visible world into our 'vibrations', the 'here' into 'the whole'; the 'friendship' with Nature; the 'transformation' of Nature into 'ourselves', the two-way interplay of our own vibrations and those of the world, the universe – all these themes are in *Aus den sieben Tagen.* And the twelfth of the Sonnets to Orpheus (First Part) might almost be a salutation to *Kurzwellen*!

Heil dem Geist, der uns verbinden mag;
denn wir leben wahrhaft in Figuren.
Und mit kleinen Schritten gehn die Uhren
neben unserm eigentlichen Tag.

Ohne unsern wahren Platz zu kennen,
handeln wir aus wirklichem Bezug.
Die Antennen fühlen die Antennen,
und die leere Ferne trag. . . .

Reine Spannung. O Musik der Kräfte!
Ist nicht durch die lässlichen Geschäfte
jede Störung von dir abgelenkt?

Selbst wenn sich der Bauer sorgt und handelt,
wo die Saat in Sommer sich verwandelt,
reicht er niemals hin. Die Erde *schenkt.*†

† A free translation of this almost untranslatable language made by J. B. Leishman runs:

Hail to the spirit able to combine!
For our lives elude us, like a figure
stared into the stars. We share a bigger,
deeper day than ticking clocks define.

We act in true relation, without any
knowledge of our real resting-place.
The antennae feel the far antennae
through the wirelessness of space. . . .

Purest tension! Harmony of forces!
Expending our dispensable resources

Aus den sieben Tagen

The theme of *Denke nichts!* reverts to nineteenth-century composers' notions. Liszt, for instance, wrote: '(music's) supremacy lies in the pure flames of emotion that beat one against another from heart to heart without the aid of reflection. . . . Only in music does feeling . . . liberate us . . . from "the demon Thought", brushing away for brief moments his yoke from our furrowed brows.'* Tchaikovsky, in describing the 'unbounded sense of bliss' he experiences when in a genuinely creative state of mind, says: 'There is something somnambulistic about this condition. "*On ne s'entend pas vivre*".'† Mahler, with characteristic introspection, wrote: 'before (the work) organises itself, builds itself up, and ferments in his (the composer's) brain, it must be preceded by much preoccupation, engrossment with self, a being-dead to the outer world'.‡ Wagner closely parallels Stockhausen's notion of the quietening of the mind in order to perceive and then to reproduce the 'vibrations' of the self and the external world with his Schopenhauer – and Buddhist – influenced 'sympathy with external things for their own sake': 'This organ of perception (the brain), which originally and in normal cases looks outward for the purpose of satisfying the wants of the will of life, receives in the case of an abnormal development such vivid and such striking impressions from outside that for a time it emancipates itself from the service of the will, which originally had fashioned it for its own ends. It thus attains to a 'will-less' – i.e. aesthetic – contemplation of the world; and these external objects, contemplated *apart from the will*, are exactly the ideal images which the artist in a manner fixes and reproduces.'§

But whereas in the nineteenth century we find a heroic gesture of idealism, with Stockhausen it is more coolly practical, apollonian rather than dionysiac in tone, and more impersonal. If Wagner also thought of himself as a vessel, he was nonetheless a highly egotistical one. Stockhausen has, like the rest of us, reacted against the megalomania, but not the essential doctrine. The most important difference, however, lies in the fact that this salutary doctrine is really 'taught' in *Aus den sieben Tagen*, and has been extended beyond the composer's domain to include (obligatorily) the performers and the listeners too.

What are we to make of these 'compositions'? Stockhausen is advocating a recipe for pure water in the context of a gourmet's recipe book. To our palates jaded with Brahms and Strauss he offers the simple sound, played from

---

we leave a silence round your instruments.

Where the seed is turning into summer
even that most constant go-and-comer,
the farmer, never reaches. Earth presents.

ibid., p. 59.

* Franz Liszt, 'Berlioz and his "Harold" Symphony', 1855. Translated by Otto Strunk in *Source Readings in Musical History*, Faber, 1950, p. 847.

† Letter dated 24 June, 1878, quoted and translated by Rosa Newmarch in *Life and Letters of P. I. Tchaikovsky*, New York, p. 306.

‡ Letter to Anna Bahr-Mildenburg, 18 July, 1896, translated by Sam Morgenstern in *Composers on Music*, Faber, 1958, p. 312.

§ Richard Wagner, *Prose Works* (vol. II) 'Opera and Drama', p. 152, translated W. A. Ellis, 1895.

the depths. To anybody meditating, or achieving what St. Teresa called the prayer of quiet, the beauty of a simple soft sound is beyond description. But then so is almost anything perceived in this state. I do not need (nor does Stockhausen) to describe the value and wonder of contemplation, that has been better done centuries ago, but such an explicit tie-up between contemplative states and musical performance or contemplative states and listening has not been recommended in such extreme terms before, though it has obviously been at the back of primitive and sacred and mantric music from the very beginning.

All music demands an imaginative response from the listener, a bell must ring inside him at every point. Coleridge said that we know a man for a poet by the fact that he makes us poets. The listener is not concerned with the sounds themselves, but with what they mean when concentrated upon or imaginatively interpreted; that is what makes it 'listening' as opposed to 'hearing', for we 'hear' sounds continually but we 'listen' to very few. The more imaginative the response from the listener and performer the better. Indeed, to take the listener's case first, one is forced to see Stockhausen's very long recent compositions as contemplative states of '*heavenly* length' as some people say of Bruckner, because from many conventional points of view they are very thin. But *can* one make an imaginative response if it seems ultimately wishful thinking? Let me give an example. A few drinks into a party you see at the other end of the room a beautiful lady. You ask someone standing next to you who she is. They tell you she is a famous Parisian courtesan, who has been the cause of three duels and a murder and

that she has just fled the country in disguise. You look at her with mounting interest. What exquisitely soft hair, what an amazing combination of refinement and sensuality, what delicate but passionate movements. When you actually discover that the lower middle-class housewife, whose most dangerous habits are bingo and telly, could yet lead you to poetic heights of imagination that were from some points of view, at least, well worth while, you realise that they had more to do with your imagination and the neighbour who had you on than with the lady herself. Beauty, we must accept, is in the ear of the listener, but when Stockhausen or any other composer gives us only indications of beauty and tells us to make ourselves especially susceptible, we quickly tire and demand that the lady really *must* be a Parisian courtesan if we are to take him at all seriously, we are not interested in mere experiments, the quest for knowledge and insight is too serious.

From the performer's point of view much the same thing is true. Imaginative collaboration is important, indispensable; and those who perform late Stockhausen obviously get enormous creative satisfaction out of so doing; but again, it is possible to get lost poetising about sounds in a way which is too subjective, too remote from the actual event, and above all, too out of touch with the musical realities the audience demands in order to get its imagination working. Group improvisation, in some form the essence of many of Stockhausen's recent works, can by definition only be either simple or chaotic in terms of musical thought, there is not time for it to be anything else. (As jazz virtuosi show, however, it can do wonders for the performers.) As soon as there is more than one person improvising, enormous simplicities or chaoses arise. There are either boringly obvious climaxes and lulls or there is a veneer of complexity which sounds all too obviously the unsatisfactory handiwork of chance. Only to the extent that functional harmony (even in the *very* broadest sense) does not matter any more are group improvisations successful, for it is strictly impossible to improvise *cogent* harmony in a group. Simultaneous intervals or controlled densities do still matter and those works such as *Adieu* and *Stimmung* in which the harmony is not improvised are therefore the most successful. But even that must (logically) be considered inferior (for all the liberation of performers etc.) to music with the 'best improvisation', thought out and written down in the leisure of the composer's workshop, and then well performed. That is why Baroque improvisation – for example, as in a Corelli violin sonata where the violinist ornaments his line furiously and the harpsichordist realises his figures with all the imagination the tempo will allow him – for all its brilliance – was eventually and progressively superseded by the exact notation of all the cleverest ideas of the harpsichordist, with other middle parts added, to create an even more complex interplay of independent life in individual parts under an overriding harmonic order.

It may be objected that the short wave radio works, for instance, are not improvisation, for the performer is following strict and difficult instructions ('imitate this short wave event etc.'). But, the number of decisions the performer has to make is literally enormous, however instinctively he may make them. As far as simultaneities are concerned, 'chance' may be a better description than 'improvised'. (It may also be objected here that Stockhausen does not claim to be the composer of these sound events – 'it is not *my* music'. That, though true, is hardly the most interesting point, which remains after every realisation: 'was it *good* music?'.) Needless to say, it has to be very good indeed to stand beside our other musical experiences, which are mostly of hearing things which we already know, for it is impossible to repeat an improvisation except on record. When we hear pieces for the fourth and fifth time or more, we are reaching to the profoundest possible musical perception because we both know the total piece and live each moment, with its 'surprises', with all the more enriched intensity. Such complex experiences are impossible with once-only pieces.

However, as an antidote to certain prevalent tendencies (dehumanisation etc.) there is much to be said for Stockhausen's 'unfinished' pieces. Because the players' musicality (intuition, spirituality) is so deeply tapped, these works sound slightly different in surface quality from any other music when well played. Such sounds could hardly be hit upon by notational means when one is using short wave radios; for instance Stockhausen's artistic flair for new sound experiences is directly related to the improvisation mentality. Think, for instance, of the effect of *Expo for 3*, performed in the Stockhausen Pavilion in the Osaka Exhibition of 1970, when you, the audience are suspended in the middle of a sphere on a sound permeable platform, surrounded by seventy loudspeakers – an idea Stockhausen wrote about in 1958, an adaptation of Frederick Kiesler's 'Endless Theatre' designs of 1924. The complexity of the short wave (received from 'the world') sounds and instrumental sounds and where they come from, the 'now' etc. is obviously what is important and significant, one would be overwhelmed by the *immediacy* of the beauty. The performers, the score, the equipment, the situation, everything is geared to that. Meanwhile sustained musical argument of the *Zeitmasze* or *Gruppen* sort is forgotten. There are many items, but few arguments, which is what I was saying about the pointillist period. A dimension considered among the most wonderful and mysterious of which the human mind is capable, is missing. Has Stockhausen turned full circle? Perhaps it is more of a spiral, and the future will bring, as happened with *Piano Piece V*, a new binding together of the individual riches collected up in the moment-form period into a more closely interacting structure where, as I said of that earlier period, the single stick which is just a single stick has been abandoned, and three sticks have been picked up and made into a triangle. The age in which we live, for musical, sociological and psychological reasons, needs more construction than destruction. It is no longer important to shout four letter words in the theatre; the breakdown of the outmoded is accomplished. The intense feelings we wish to express must be bound together more coherently and imaginatively than ever before if we want to say anything new. But if one had been writing around the time of Stravinsky's *Rite of Spring*, Schoenberg's *Erwartung* and Webern's Op. 6 one would probably have said exactly the opposite. Stockhausen's prophecy that as we move into the age of Aquarius we will jettison the intellectual attitudes prevalent since the time of the ancient Greeks for the new spiritual and mystical attitudes of which he is a herald elicits a broader view of history than I feel qualified to pronounce upon; but as a hopeful sign that Stockhausen's creative spiral may be twisting, and considered thought may be blended in a new synthesis with Aquarian experience, I will quote a few sentences from a 1971 interview: 'The next step I have to take is to find out how to superimpose several layers of more or less determinate quality, so that at a given moment one group will play completely intuitively. But what they play will be related to what they hear played by a group whose music is completely predetermined. Let's say that I want to have five or six fast chords in a row. This will never come about in an eternity in an intuitive group, because human minds are never automatically synchronised. On the other hand, collective intuition produces qualities that you can't otherwise achieve. When musicians are not too much bound by instructions, then they react to the sound itself. They could never say why they did it that way. They just did it in the moment they were listening.'*

It seems a reasonable and practical distinction to make between what the performer likes or wills, and what 'suggests itself to him', without going as far as Cage's total banishment of personality in his philosophies of self-subjugation to the impersonal dictates of chance and silence. (Cage's ideas, incidentally, may have suggested a great deal of Stockhausen's thought, the seeds of nearly all of them are to be found in Cage's Darmstadt lectures and

* Interview with Peter Heyworth, *Music and Musicians*, May, 1971, p. 34.

articles of the late fifties – which is not to deny Stockhausen's originality in developing them.) Where these sounds come from that 'suggest themselves' – from the un- or super-conscious, the air around us, viruses from another planet (Stockhausen suggests this too) – is inevitably a matter of dispute; the important thing for Stockhausen is that we react Platonically and progress towards a higher state of consciousness, eventually to a new evolutionary stage not dissimilar to that envisaged by Chardin. It is a wonderful, heroic idea, and I believe in it almost as much as the thousands of young musicians and non-musicians who pack out Stockhausen's concerts and for whom he is a cultural, almost extramusical, guru. But there lurks also the nagging question as to whether this is not the same tragic situation as that which obtained in Schoenberg's *Moses und Aron*. Moses lacks the form to convey the vision. Is not the closed form, the object, the mysteriously resonant *symbol* still the only hope for storming heaven? A state in which one is susceptible to the divinity, as Haydn put it, can be induced by music; but the music should preferably do the inducing itself, i.e. should be excellent by our criteria in a purely musical (formal) sense and become more and more fascinating as acquaintance increases and every detail becomes distinct in the memory, otherwise we must say that it is not the music itself that is having an effect upon us, but rather the lectures, articles, philosophies and day dreams with which it has been plastered. The music *per se* is in this case unnecessary to the blessed state. It seems that in the indeterminate, ultra-intuitive works of Stockhausen one runs the risk of incoherence and non-communication: the trance is beautiful, but it is all and everything; however crude the sounds, in this state they are seen, as Cage would say, as the Buddha. So it is not music itself that Stockhausen is talking about but our interpretation of that music as listeners (or performer-listeners). There really is a distinction between patterns of sonic relationships on the one hand and what we make of them on the other, however buried in centuries of confusion this distinction might be; and the first step towards understanding the metaphysics of music is to draw it.

Appendix (1972)

Mantra for two pianists represents a return to the 'personal', an assertion of the individual mind rather than a sinking into the collective spirit. It was written in two months, June to August, 1970, and is a lengthy, fully notated and systematically complex work. Each performer plays also a woodblock and a set of crotales. If this suggests similarities with *Refrain*, then one is quite mistaken. Each work is by axiom uniquely different from all others. In addition there are two sine-wave producing oscillators for whom parts appear in the score. Their pitches are sent to a ring-modulator with the piano's sounds and ring modulated with them, the result being sent out into loudspeakers. This means that an entirely new 'system'* of harmony is created in that each note of the chromatic scale, when ring modulated with a held pitch, produces two other pitches (the sum tone and the difference tone) which are more or less consonant depending on the interval of the piano's note from the sine wave pitch. For instance, a chromatic scale against Piano 1's first sine tone produces the following approximate 'harmony' (Ex. 51): showing that the subdominant (D), the dominant (E) and above all the unison and octave (A) produce especially euphonious harmony, clearly arranging the twelve available pitch classes in a hierarchy dominated by the current sine tone 'tonic'. Each of the twelve degrees of any 'tonality' has a distinctive and unique sound. In the tonal system proper, the same pitch (identical sound) can belong to any of twelve (or twenty-four) tonalities and often to several at once, each on a different level of background determination. Serial and atonal music ('pantonal' music included) sacrifices this multivalence of meaning except in near-foreground structure and substitutes other types of meaning. Now, in *Mantra*, we see an interesting attempt to bring back the hierarchisation of tonality, but because there is only one level of 'tonic' – each note says very definitely by its colour 'I belong to such and such a tonic' – the richness of tonal multivalence is impossible. But there is the increased richness of meaning resulting from the addition of tonicality to the other meanings of the type we normally associate with Stockhausen's determinate music. He has used an additional stratum of meaning, this tonicality, to *define* the large-scale serial structure of the piece. The 'mantra' series upon which everything is based is played, with its inversion, by the sine wave oscillators over the twelve-plus-

* i.e. it is globally true for this piece.

Appendix

Ex. 51

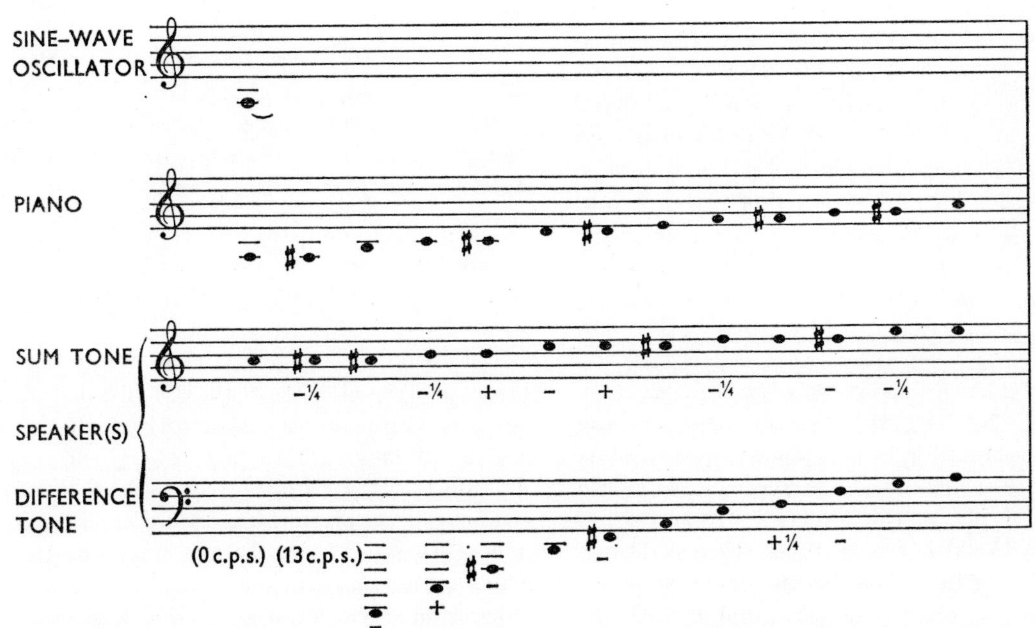

one sections, with one note plus its inversion per section. The mantra or series and its accompanying inversion are as follows:

Ex. 52

So, except for the first section, the eighth, and the long thirteenth section, there are two 'tonics' running in each section, a complexity which reduces possible conflict between tonal structure on one level and 'serial structure on another',* and at the same time emphasises a very background tonic of A, which is much clearer than any other tonic except E flat by virtue of the oscillators' unisons.

On the microcosmic level the mantra is

* See discussion of this in chapter 4, '. . . how time passes . . .', p. 31.

articulated by thirteen stylistic characteristics which may be followed from bar 3 of Example 53. In this serialisation of 'motives' *Mantra* reverts to the technique first tried in *Formel* nineteen years earlier. They are: 1(A) regular repetition, 2(B) sharp off-beat accent, 3(G sharp) normal, 4(E) grace-note upbeat around a central note, 5(F + D) tremolo with next pitch, 6(D) note with chord, 7(G) loud double-attack, 8(E flat) grace note link with previous note, 9(D flat) staccato, 10(C) irregular repetition – parent of 'morse code' style, 11(B flat) embryo trill, 12(G flat) *sfp* mode of attack, 13(A) note accompanied by arpeggio (Ex. 53).

These thirteen characteristics also in turn characterise the thirteen sections on the macrocosmic level, accompanying the slow sequence of sine tones as they accompanied the fast sequence of the pitches in Example 53. Within the thirteen sections there is also a sequence of the other stylistic characteristics, thus section one, though dominated throughout by characteristic *1* (regularly repeated notes) treats also characteristic *2* in bars 12–13 (13 beats), characteristic *3* in bars 14–19½ (26 beats), characteristic *4* in 19½–21 (13 beats), characteristic *5* in 22–25 (13 beats), *6* in 26–29 (13 beats), *7* in 30–38 (13 + 13 beats), *8* in 39–46 (26 beats), *9* in 47–52 (26 beats), *10* in 53–55 (22 beats, slower), *11* in 56–58 (22 beats), *12* in 59–61 (16 beats), *13* in 62–64 (28 beats). (Note the prevalence of *13-beat* microcosms.)

Throughout the first section, the *cantus* of repeated notes follows exactly the duration proportions of the original mantra (Example 53), but using semibreves as units instead of crotchets. Likewise there are all sorts of

diminutions of the duration set (see Example 54).

Stockhausen also uses thirteen different types of scale through which to filter his mantra scales. These scales are generated by widening the intervals of the mantra, as is shown by the two excerpts in Exx. 53 and 54.

Mantra is different from Stockhausen's earlier, determinate music in many ways. The form is more immediately recognisable as stemming from a single idea than ever before, yet the variety of texture is greater than in any piano piece, and the element of theatre (for instance when the two players make quasi-Noh vocal and woodblock calls to each other), the ring-modulation, the crotales, when added to the richness of purely musical thought, all make it a synthesis of more diverse invention than Stockhausen has previously achieved. It is an expression of Stockhausen's 'vibrations within vibrations' theory on a grand and colourful scale – with the largest mantra in the sine-wave-oscillator-induced succession of 'tonics', the next largest in the crotale part, which gets through the mantra and (subsequently) its inversion during the course of the piece, the next in the 'cantus firmus' mantra running through each region, and the rest at various speeds in the twelve short representations within each of these regions. There are in all 13 × 12 = 156 appearances of the mantra before the 'coda' on the final sine tone unison A. This coda in rapid semiquavers flees through the entire 156 mantras in about four minutes. Though the pitch currency is virtually debased to mere texture, there is a climactic excitement about the passage with its savagely placed chordal interjections which, like the climax of *Gruppen*, is hard to resist.

Ex. 53

schnell
langsam
Prime: 1–4 5–6 7–10 11–13
dicht repetieren
rit.
Prime: 1
Inversion: 5+6
(chordal display of the mantra's partitioning)
(start of characteristic style of the first region)
WOOD BLOCK
CYMBALES ANTIQUES
Prime: 1
220
poco sfz

Ex. 54

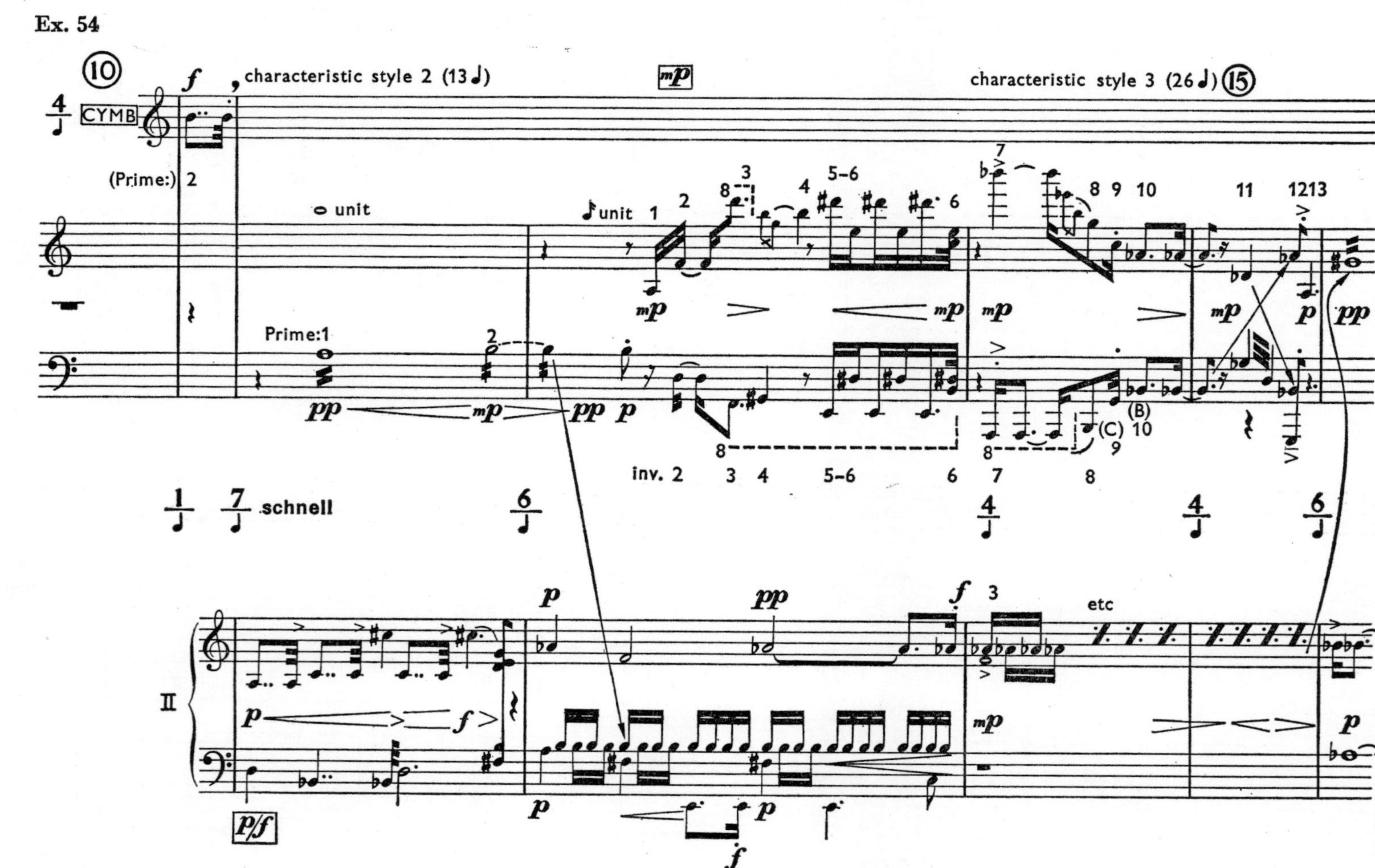

CYMB
characteristic style 2 (13 ♩)
(Prime:) 2
unit
Prime:1
unit
inv. 2
schnell
characteristic style 3 (26 ♩)
etc

Appendix

Ex. 55

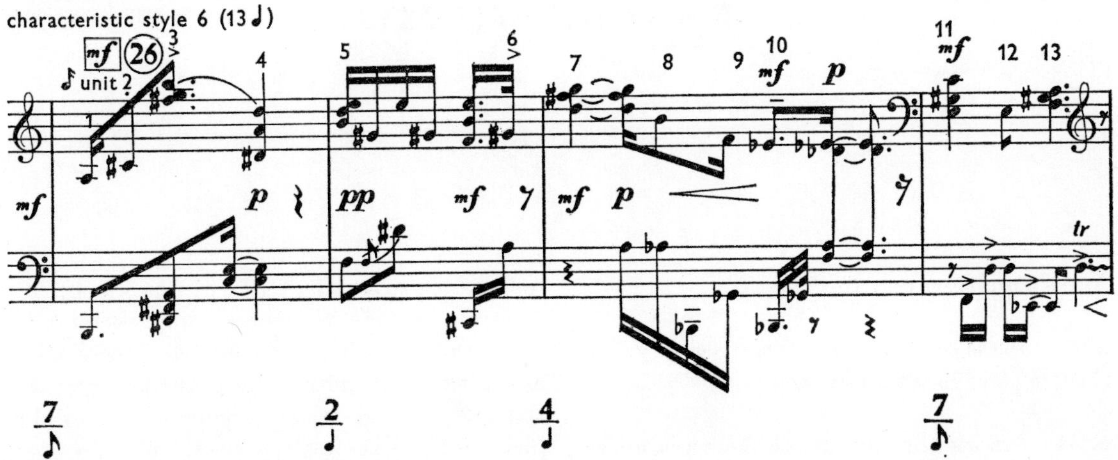

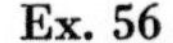

Ex. 56

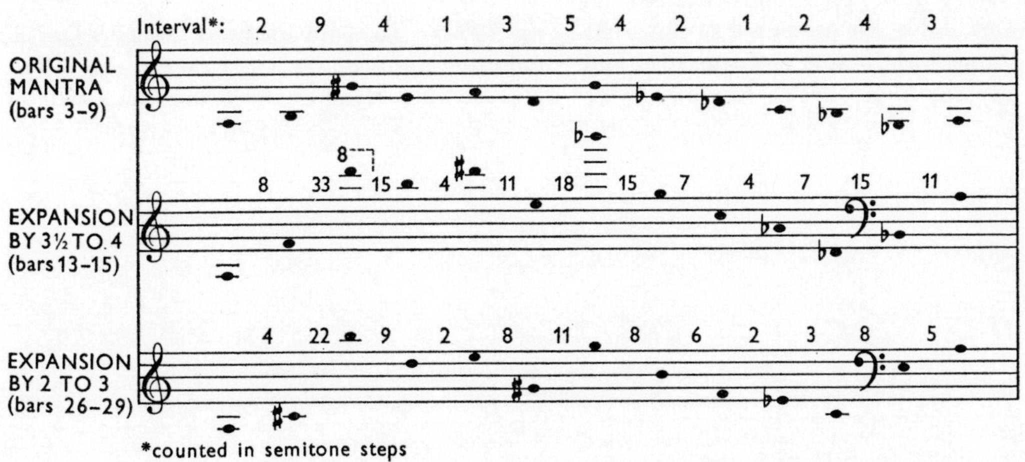

Appendix (1974)

Notes supplementary to the text:

p. 23 *Herbstmusik*, written very recently, is a theatre piece in four movements.

p. 34 *Inori* is the score Stockhausen is working on at the present time of writing. It uses the logarithmic tempo scale in a much more complex manner than *Gruppen* (much quicker changes), but the material itself is rhythmically simpler.

pp. 38–42 *Piano Pieces V–VIII* stem from an overall background plan of a 6 × 6 magic square and 5 derived squares. Stockhausen has, however, moved such a long distance from that background to the presented surface that analysis along such lines is problematical and aurally unrewarding. Drastic revisions were made to nearly all of the pieces. In *V*, for example, all the character-groups belong to the revision; only relatively long notes with attendant grace notes were present at first. In the first versions almost every aspect of the pieces is based on these squares, but of the final published versions, it is only *VIII* that remains fairly close to the original serial conception.

p. 63 Although the band widths are globally fixed over a group, they often have inner movement. A strongly directional spiralling towards the next bandwidth can sometimes be heard; for instance in the descending groups 62–65.

pp. 105–6 The conversations are with David Johnson, Stockhausen's assistant in the WDR studios when *Hymnen* was being composed.

Bibliography

BOOKS

JONATHAN COTT, *Stockhausen – Conversations with the Composer*, Robson Books, 1974.

K. STOCKHAUSEN, *Texte*, DuMont Dokumente, Verlag M. Dumont Schauberg, Köln, Volumes One and Two, 1964. Volume Three, 1971.

KARL H. WÖRNER, *Karlheinz Stockhausen, Werk & Wollen 1950–1962*, Kontrapunkte, Band 6, P. J. Tonger Musikverlag. Rodenkirchen/Rhein, 1963.
Also translated into English by G. W. Hopkins as *Stockhausen: Life and Work*, with translator's preface and new material. Faber and Faber, London; University of California Press, Berkeley and Los Angeles, 1973.

ARTICLES

CORNELIUS CARDEW, 'Report on Stockhausen's *Carré*', *The Musical Times*, vol. 102 (1961), pp. 619–22, 698–700.

JONATHAN COTT, 'Conversation with Stockhausen' in *Rolling Stone*, 8th July 1971.

HUGH DAVIES, 'Working with Stockhausen', *Composer 27* (1968), pp. 8–11.

ADRIAN D. FOKKER, 'Wherefore, and Why?' *Die Reihe*, vol. 8, pp. 68–79.

JONATHAN HARVEY, 'Stockhausen: Theory and Music', *The Music Review*, vol. 29 (1968), pp. 130–41.

SEPPO HEIKINHEIMO, 'Stockhausen's *Kontakte*', *University of Helsinki.*

PETER HEYWORTH, 'Spiritual Dimensions' (interview with Stockhausen), *Music and Musicians*, May 1971, pp. 32–43.

G. W. HOPKINS, 'Stockhausen, form, and sound', *The Musical Times*, vol. 109 (1968), pp. 60–2.

ERHARD KARKOSCHKA, 'Stockhausens Theorien', *Melos*, vol. 32 (1965), pp. 5–13.

MAX EUGEN KELLER, 'Gehörte und komponierte Struktur in Stockhausens *Kreuzspiel*', *Melos* I, 1972. p. 10.

GOTTFRIED MICHAEL KOENIG, 'Commentary on Stockhausen's ". . . how time passes . . .", on Fokker's "wherefore and why?" and on present musical practice', *Die Reihe*, vol. 8, pp. 80–98.

ROBIN MACONIE, 'Stockhausen's *Setz die Segel zur Sonne*', *Tempo 92* (1970), pp. 30–2.

ROBIN MACONIE, 'Stockhausens *Microphonie I*', *Perspectives of New Music*, 10, 1972, p. 92.

ROBIN MACONIE, '*Momente* in London', *Tempo* 104, 1973, pp. 32–3.

GENEVIEVE MARCUS, 'Stockhausen's *Zeitmasse*', *The Music Review*, vol. 29 (1968), pp. 142–56.

BROCK MCELHERAN, 'Preparing Stockhausen's *Momente*', *Perspectives of New Music*, Fall-Winter 1965, pp. 33–8.

JORGE PEIXINHO, 'Stockhausen em Paris', *Coloquio artes* II/6, February 1972, pp. 53–4 (Summary in French).

K. RITZEL, *Musik für ein Haus*, Schott, Mainz.

H. W. SCHMIDT and DR. KIRCHMEYER, *Von Webern bis Stockhausen*, Verlag Gerig, Cologne.

DIETER SCHNEBEL, 'Karlheinz Stockhausen', *Die Reihe*, vol. 4, pp. 121–35.

ROGER SMALLEY, 'Stockhausen's *Gruppen*', *The Musical Times*, vol. 108 (1967), pp. 794–7.

ROGER SMALLEY, 'Stockhausen's Piano Pieces, some notes for the listener', *The Musical Times*, vol. 110 (1969), pp. 30–2.

ROGER SMALLEY, 'Stockhausen and development', *The Musical Times*, April 1970, pp. 379–81.

ROGER SMALLEY, 'Momente', *The Musical Times*, January 1974, pp. 23–8 (part 1) and April 1974, pp. 289–95 (part 2).

KARLHEINZ STOCKHAUSEN, Articles in English in *Die Reihe*:
'Actualia', vol. 1, pp. 45–51.
'For the 15th of September, 1955', vol. 2, pp. 37–9.
'Structure and Experiential Time', vol. 2, pp. 64–75.
'. . . how time passes . . .', vol. 3, pp. 10–40.
'Two lectures: I Electronic and Instrumental Music', vol. 5, pp. 59–66; II 'Music in Space', pp. 67–82.
'Music and Speech', vol. 6, pp. 40–64.

'The Concept of Unity in Electronic Music', translated by Elaine Barkin in *Perspectives of New Music*, Fall 1962, pp. 39–48.

'A Mouth Piece', 'Not a Special Day', 'Charter for Youth'; three articles translated by Harry Partridge which first appeared in the American magazine *The Composer*, reprinted in *Feedback*, a pamphlet edited by Richard Toop, together with Stockhausen's programme note for *Mantra*, produced to coincide with Stockhausen's visit to England in April-May 1971. Published by Robert Slotover (Allied Artists).

Bibliography

'Elektronische Musik und Automatik', *Melos*, vol. 32 (1965), pp. 337–44.
'Plus Minus auf vierzehn Notenblättern', *Melos*, vol. 33 (1966), pp. 144–5.
'Mikrophonie I und Mikrophonie II', *Melos*, vol. 33 (1966), pp. 354–8.
'Musik für die Beethovenhalle', *Melos*, vol. 36 (1969), p. 514.

Discography

This list of all the available gramophone records of his music does not group the works according to the compositional processes involved: the headings are intended to give only approximately the instrumental/electronic media for which the works are written. Further details of instrumentation and a complete list of the published scores are available from UNIVERSAL EDITION.

Abbreviations:

Ph.	Philips	RCA. (It.)	RCA Italy
Col.	Columbia	(Lon.)	RCA Victrola (London)
M.	Mainstream	DGG.	Deutsche Grammophon
V.	Vega (French)	W.	Wergo (French)
Hz.	Hörzu (German)	Vox (can)	Vox (candide)
CBS. (NY.) (Pa.)	Columbia Broadcasting System (New York or Paris)		

PIANO MUSIC

Klavierstücke I–XI	Aloys Kontarsky	CBS. (NY.) 32 21 00 08
	Aloys Kontarsky	CBS. (Pa.) S 77209
Klavierstück VI	(early version) David Tudor	V. C 30 A278
Klavierstück VIII	David Burge	Vox (can) STGBY 637
Klavierstück IX	Marie-Françoise Bucquet	Ph. 6500 101
Klavierstück X	Frederic Rzewski	W. 60010
	Frederic Rzewski	Hz. SHZW 903 BL
Klavierstück XI	Marie-Françoise Bacquet	Pa. 6500 101

INSTRUMENTAL/ORCHESTRAL

Carré	NDR. Choir and Orchestra, dir. Kagel, Stockhausen, Markowski, Gielen.	DGG. ST. 137002

Discography

Work	Performers	Recording
Gruppen	Cologne Radio S.O. dir. Stockhausen Maderna and Gielen.	DGG. ST. 137002
Refrain	Aloys Kontarsky, Christoph Caskel, Bernhard Kontarsky.	Ti. 58001 (series 2000)
Refrain	Aloys Kontarsky, Christoph Caskel, Stockhausen.	Vox (can) STGBY 638
	as above	Fratelli Fabri Editori mm. 1048 (Vox)
Zeitmasze	dir. Pierre Boulez	V. C30 A 139
	dir. Robert Craft	Ph. A01 488 L
	dir. Robert Craft	CBS. 32 160 154 (Odyssey series)
	Heinz Holliger and members of Danzi Quintet	Ph. 6500 261
Zyklus	Christoph Caskel	Ti. 58001 (series 2000)
	Caskel, Max Neuhaus	W. 60010
	Caskel (same as W. 60010)	Hz. SHZW 903 BL
	Neuhaus	Col. 7139
	Gualda	Erato STU 70603 (France)
	Yamaguchi	Sonc. 16 012 (Japan)
Kontra-Punkte	Bruno Maderna (cond)	RCA. (It) SLD 61005 (3)
	Bruno Maderna (cond)	RCA. (Lon) VICS 1239
	Pierre Boulez	V. C 30 A 66 (France)
Momente	WDR. Choir and Orchestra, dir. Stockhausen (M. Arroyo, soprano)	W. 60024 (also Nonesuch)
Stimmung (six vocalists)	'Collegium Vocale Köln'	DGG. 2543003

ELECTRONIC MUSIC

Electronic Studies I and *II*	DGG. LP 16133
Gesang der Jünglinge	DGG. LP 16133 (monaural)
	DGG. 138811 (stereophonic)

Kontakte (electronic version)	WDR., Stockhausen realisation	DGG. 138811
Telemusik	NHK. Tokyo, Stockhausen realisation	DGG. 643546
Hymnen	WDR., Stockhausen realisation	DGG. 139421–2

LIVE ELECTRONIC MUSIC

Solo	Vinko Globokar, trombone	DGG. ST. 104 992
Spiral	Michael Vetter, elec. recorder	W. 325
	Michael Vetter, elec. recorder	Hz. SHZW. 903 BL
(two versions)	Bojé, Eötvös	Electrola C 165–02 313/14
	Heinz Holliger, oboe	D 99 2561 109
Kontakte	David Tudor, C. Caskel, Stockhausen.	W. 60 009
	as above, but with A. Kontarsky and not D. Tudor.	Vox (can) STGBY 638
Prozession	Alfred Alings, Rolf Gehlhaar, Johannes Fritsch, Harald Bojé, Aloys Kontarsky, Stockhausen.	Vox (can) New York CE. 31001; London STGBY 615
	as above (same performance)	CBS. (Paris) S 77230
	as above (different performance)	Fratelli Fabri Editori mm. 1098 (Vox)
Kurzwellen (two versions)	two discs, dir. Stockhausen Johannes Fritsch, Aloys Kontarsky, Alfred Alings, Rolf Gehlhaar, Harald Bojé, Stockhausen.	DGG. 2707045
Mikrophonie I	A. Kontarsky, Alfred Alings J. Fritsch, H. Bojé, K. Stockhausen, H. Davies, J. Spek.	CBS. (NY.) 32 110044 and CBS. (Pa.) S 77230
Mikrophonie II	Members of the WDR. Choir, Schernus, A. Kontarsky, J. Fritsch, K. Stockhausen.	See *Mikrophonie I* (both on one disc)

Discography

Mixtur	Ensemble Hudba Dnesca, dir. Ladislav Kupkovič (WDR).	DGG. ST. 643546
Setz die Segel zur Sonne *Verbindung* (both from *Aus den sieben Tagen*)	Bojé, Alings, Gehlhaar, Kontarsky, Clark, Fritsch, Portal, Drovet, Stockhausen.	Musique Vivante MV. 30795
Kurzwellen mit Beethoven: Stockhoven–Beethausen Opus 1970	A. Kontarsky, Harald Bojé, Rolf Gehlhaar, Johannes Fritsch, Stockhausen.	DGG. 139461
Mantra	Alfons and Aloys Kontarsky.	DGG. 2530 208
Unbegrenzt and *Es* (both from *Aus den sieben Tagen*)	Two discs, V. Globokar (trombone), C. R. Alzina (piano), J. F. Jenny-Clark (D-B), J. P. Drouet (perc.), M. Portal (saxophone, flute, clarinet), J. G. Fritsch (viola), K. Stockhausen (speaking voice, sirens, short wave radio, filters and volume controls).	'Nuits de la Fondation Maeght' (St. Paul)
Aus den sieben Tagen (all except *Oben und Unten*, *Litanei* and *Ankunft*)	Various musicians	DGG. 2720 073
Pole	Bojé, Eötvös	Electrola C 165–02 313/14 (two discs including *Spiral*)
Japan	Bojé, Eötvös, Caskel	
Wach	Bojé, Eötvös, Caskel	

COLLECTION

Greatest hits of Karlheinz Stockhausen	*Stimmung*, *Kurzwellen*, *Gruppen*, *Mantra* – recordings are all re-issues of experts from the above.	DGG. 2612 023 (2 records)

Works by Karlheinz Stockhausen

(Student works include: *Drei Lieder* for alto and chamber orchestra, *Sonata* for violin and piano, *Drei Chöre*, *Vier Chöre*.)

1951 No. $\frac{1}{7}$ *Kreuzspiel* for oboe, bass clarinet, piano and percussion (3 players)
1951 No. $\frac{1}{6}$ *Formel* for orchestra
1952 No. $\frac{1}{5}$ *Étude* (musique concrète)
1952 No. $\frac{1}{4}$ *Spiel* for orchestra
1952 No. $\frac{1}{3}$ *Schlagquartett* for piano and 3 × 2 timpani
1952 No. $\frac{1}{2}$ *Punkte* for orchestra (see new version 1962)
1952–3 No. 1 *Kontra-Punkte* for ten instruments
1952–3 No. 2 *Piano Pieces I–IV*
1953 No. 3/i *Study I* (electronic music)
1954 No. 3/ii *Study II* (electronic music)
1954–5 No. 4 *Piano Pieces V–X* (*IX* and *X* not written out until 1961)
1955–6 No. 5 *Zeitmasze* for five woodwinds
1955–7 No. 6 *Gruppen* for three orchestras
1956 No. 7 *Piano Piece XI*
1955–6 No. 8 *Gesang der Jünglinge* (electronic music)
1959 No. 9 *Zyklus* for one percussionist
1959–60 No. 10 *Carré* for four orchestras and choirs
1959 No. 11 *Refrain* for three players
1959–60 No. 12 *Kontakte* for electronic sounds, also with piano, percussion
1961 *Originale* (musical theater)
1961 *Piano Piece VI* substantially revised
1954–61 No. 4 *Piano Pieces IX* and *X*
1962 *Punkte* (revised)
1962–4 No. 13 *Momente* for soprano, four choir groups, 13 instrumentalists
1963 No. 14 *Plus Minus* 2 × 7 pages for realisation
1964 No. 15 *Mikrophonie I* for tamtam, two microphones, two filters and potentiometers (6 players)

Works

1964 No. 16 *Mixtur* for orchestra, sine-wave generators and ring-modulators
1965 No. 17 *Mikrophonie II* for choir, Hammond organ, and four ring-modulators
1965–6 No. 18 *Stop* for orchestra
1965–6 No. 19 *Solo* for melody instrument and tape-delay system
1966 No. 20 *Telemusik* (electronic music)
1966 No. 21 *Adieu* for wind quintet
1966–7 No. 22 *Hymnen* electronic and 'concrete' music, also with four players, third 'region' also with orchestra
1967 No. 23 *Prozession* for tamtam, viola, electronium, piano, two filters and potentiometers
1968 No. 24 *Stimmung* for six vocalists
1968 No. 25 *Kurzwellen* for tamtam, viola, electronium, piano, four short wave radios, filters and potentiometers
1968 No. 26 *Aus den sieben Tagen* – 15 compositions, May 1968
1968 No. 27 *Spiral* for one player or singer with short wave radio
1969 No. 18½ *Stop* (Paris version) for orchestra
1969 No. 28 *Fresco* for 4 orchestral groups
1969–70 No. 29 *Pole* for 2
1969–70 No. 30 *Expo* for 3
1968–70 No. 31 *Für Kommende Zeiten*: 17 texts of Intuitive Music:
- *Kommunication* for small ensemble
- *Über die Grenze* for smallish ensemble
- *Übereinstimmung* for ensemble
- *Verkürzung*
- *Verlängerung*
- *Intervall* for piano with four hands, to be played with closed eyes
- *Zugvogel* for ensemble
- *Anhalt* for small ensemble
- *Ausserhalb* for small ensemble
- *Innerhalb* for small ensemble
- *Schwingung* for ensemble
- *Spektren* for small ensemble
- *Wellen* for small ensemble
- *Japan* for ensemble
- *Vorahnung* for 4–7
- *Ceylon* for small ensemble
- *Wach* for ensemble

1970 No. 32 *Mantra* for two pianists

1971 No. 33	*Sternklang* Park-music for 5 groups
1971 No. 34	*Trans* for orchestra
1971 No. 35	*Alphabet for Liège*
1971 No. 35½	*Am Himmel wandere ich* (Indianer-Lieder)
1972 No. 36	*Ylem* for 19 or more players/singers
1972 No. 13	*Momente* ('Bonn Version' – all the 'D' moments and the 'I(k)' moment newly composed)
1974 No. 37	*Inori, Adorations for soloist and orchestra*